Typecasting

by Robert Stadler

This exhibition is as much about furniture as it is about us. By presenting objects as characters in a film-set-like display, *Typecasting* reflects contemporary modes of self-staging as well as the strategies of collecting 'friends' and 'likes' on social media. Inspired by the related strategy of joining various 'communities', the 200 objects and furnishings in this exhibition have been combined into nine different groups: the *Communals*, *Compulsive Organizers*, *Slashers*, *Dreamers*, *Beauty Contestants*, *Dating Site Encounters*, *Spartans*, *Restless*, *Athletes*.

Along with its practical task, furniture has always had a representational function. As such, chairs can typically be read as personalities or portraits. This structure by community not only emphasises ideological convictions, behavioural traits and stylistic affinities, but also offers a new view of the broad range of objects Vitra has contributed to design. As a transhistorical, non-hierarchical presentation, *Typecasting* freely combines different object typologies chosen from Vitra's present and past output, from special editions and prototypes.

The objects that are part of the *Communals* occupy a special position in the exhibition. Firstly, since they can accommodate groups of people, they are by definition larger than most of the traditional furniture. Secondly, the group comprises six new design studies specially commissioned for *Typecasting*. Even if these furniture items were not necessarily conceived for such a purpose, they offer an ideal platform, not only for gathering but also for posing, which cannot be a coincidence in the selfie era. The *Communals* are also a good example illustrating the function of the above-mentioned transhistorical approach. Various ideas such as communal living keep on popping up in history as happened as early as the reform era of the 1930s and then again during the hippie era of the 1960s. Even if it might appear that the co-living-and-working trends are new, pieces like Verner Panton's Living Tower (1969) show that such concepts were not invented today.

Next to the actual exhibited objects there are three big LED walls displaying a slow, looping film of the same objects thus enhancing the idea of a continuity of ideas and shapes in time. The objects are filmed by six cameras controlled by a permanently on-site camera team, broadcasting the video footage in real time. Strong zooms and unusual perspectives blur the perceptual line between physical reality and digital imagery.

Looking at familiar objects through the lens of self-staging and image cultivation aims to sharpen the understanding of furniture's role in defining our personal and social profiles.

Vitra Introduction

In its first presentation at Milan's La Pelota hall–during the Salone del Mobile in 2005–Vitra showed the breadth of its product range in an installation by Ronan and Erwan Bouroullec. The 2018 presentation was intended to offer a look simultaneously at the history of the Vitra project, its actual manifestations, and also some future-oriented concepts. The idea of sharing space in homes and offices–communal living and working–has been a subject of research at Vitra for some time now and the 2018 installation would need to reflect this.

With this briefing in mind the question was who could curate this exhibition. Robert Stadler was the choice. Robert Stadler bridges disciplines, as he works as designer, artist and curator. Also he had never collaborated with Vitra before and would therefore have a fresh, an outsider's view.

Robert Stadler suggested analysing and organising the exhibition on Vitra's body of design not based on a chronology or the usual categories home, office, public space, but on the concept of objects as representatives of social communities. It was clear from the beginning that the link of products to specific communities was not based on objective criteria, but on poetic intuition with ironic undertones, the intention being to sharpen our understanding of the social role of design and particularly furniture. He gave the exhibition the title *Typecasting* and created nine communities, the central one–in line with Vitra's original briefing–being devoted to the *Communals*. In this category, Ronan and Erwan Bouroullec, Konstantin Grcic, Edward Barber and

Jay Osgerby, Robert Stadler, and Commonplace Studio presented their designs for a new typology, the 'Communal Sofa', along with past proposals, such as the Living Tower of Verner Panton from 1969.

So, in the expansive Pelota arena, a panorama of 200 objects unfolded–including successful designs, interesting flops, forgotten pieces and innovative models–and Vitra was portrayed in surprising new ways. Identifying oneself with specific objects and belonging to chosen communities are essential strategies for cultivating and projecting a desired self-image. The installation reflects this new reality by presenting the objects as personalities who identify with specific communities.

The reception of the *Typecasting* exhibition was mixed. For some it was the highlight of the Salone 2018, while others wondered what this strange mix of products was all about. Vitra welcomes controversy that stimulates the design discourse.

It did. The observation that furniture and chairs in particular have a double life as useful tools and representations of the user is of course not new. However, the emphasis on the latter function has probably never been expressed as dramatically as in *Typecasting* and in the designers' discussions which took place on the sidelines of the exhibition the question whether the role of the image of an object (driven by social media) rather than the object itself now determines its place in the market and as a consequence guides the design process was identified as one of the great challenges of designing today.

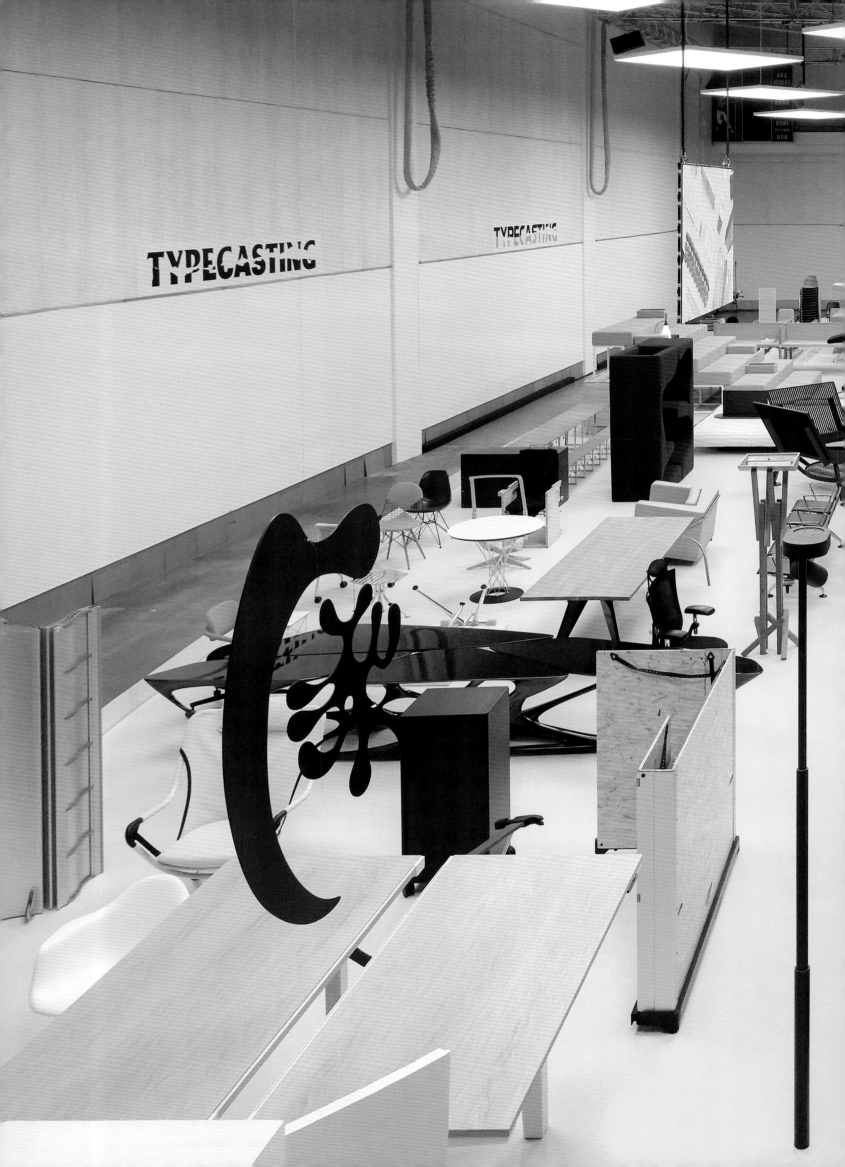

TYPECAS

ECASTING

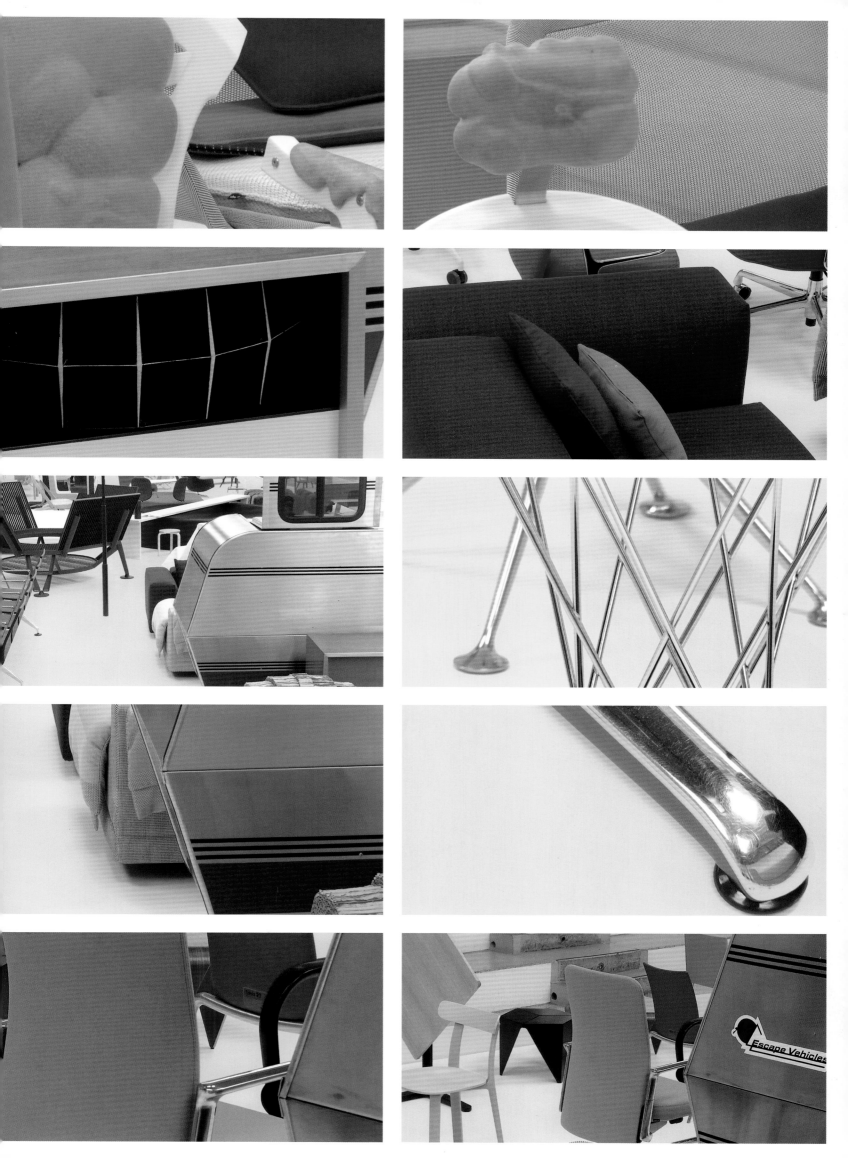

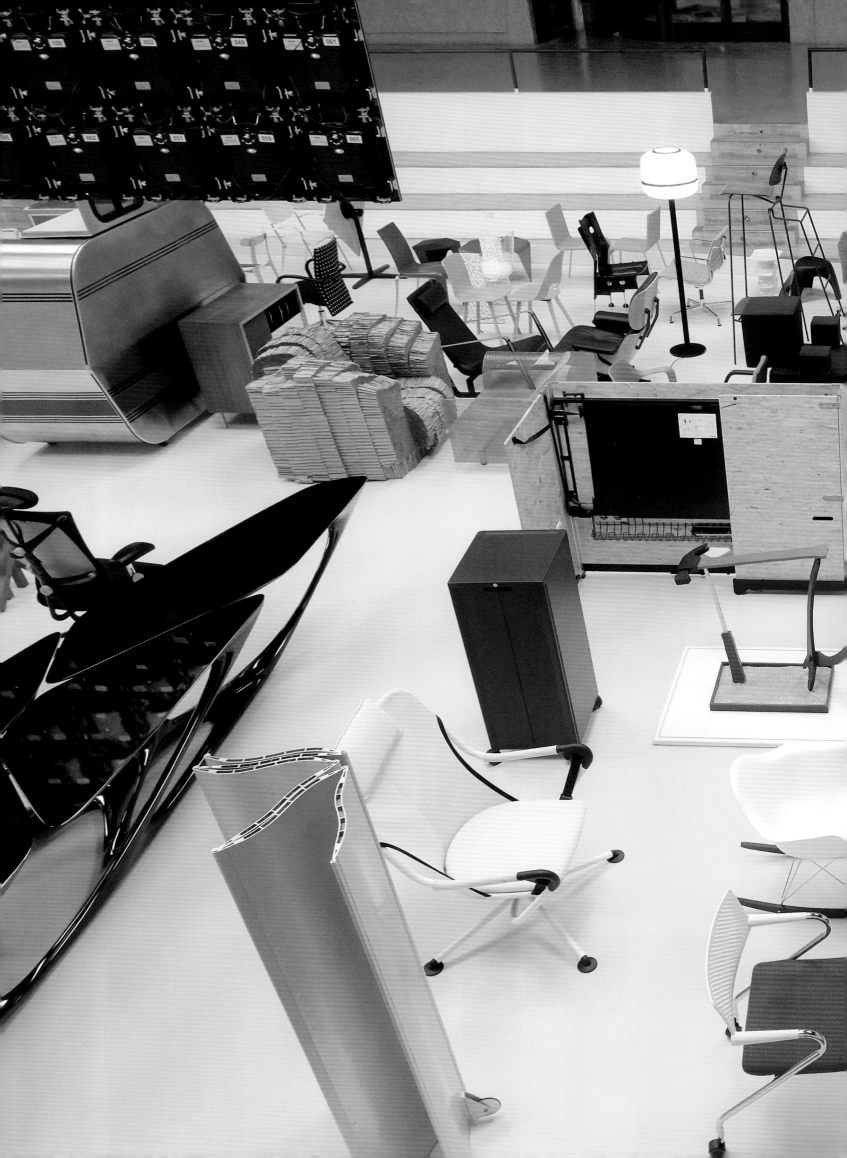

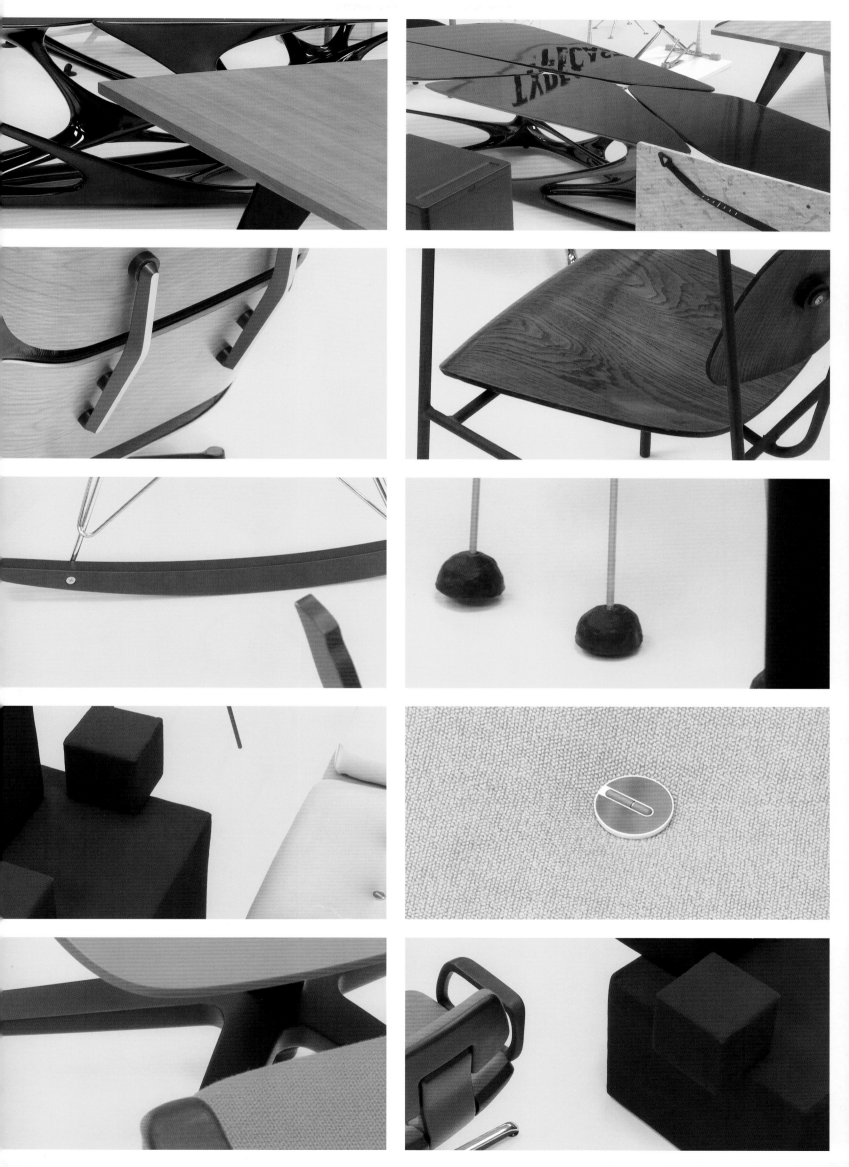

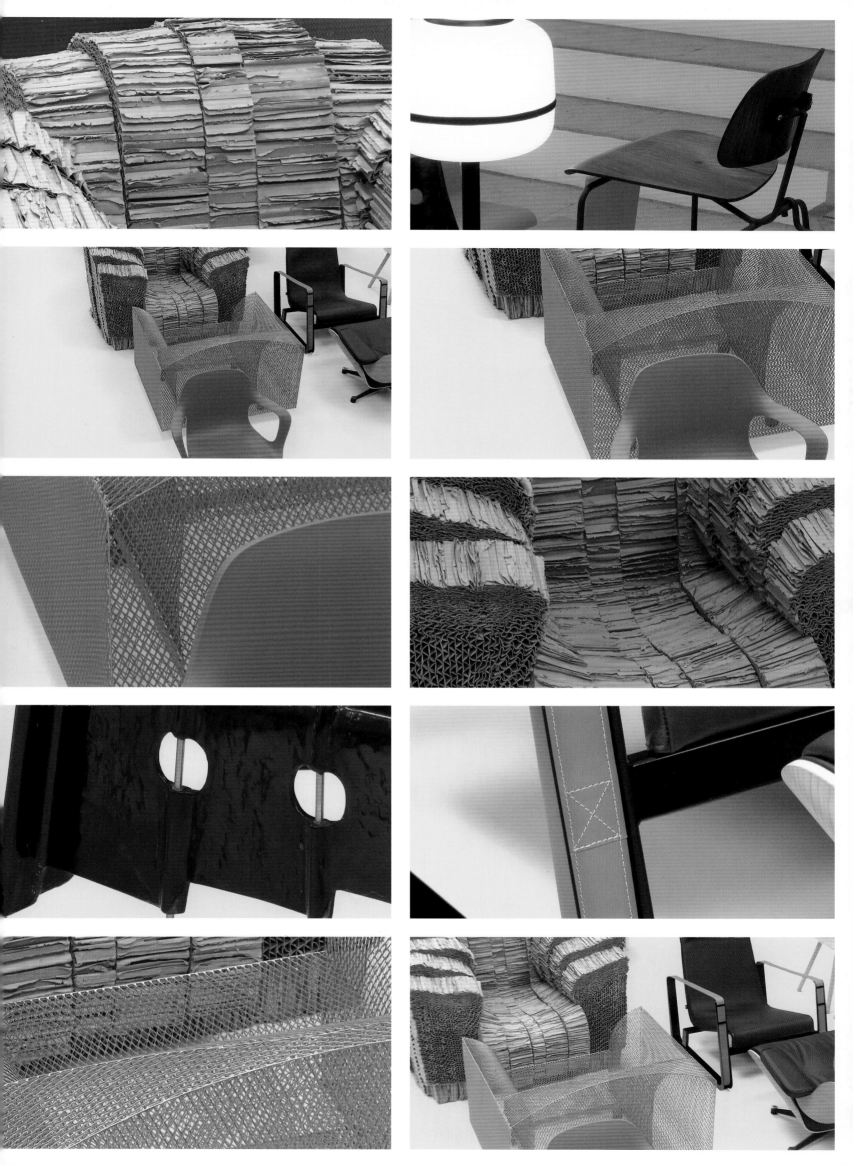

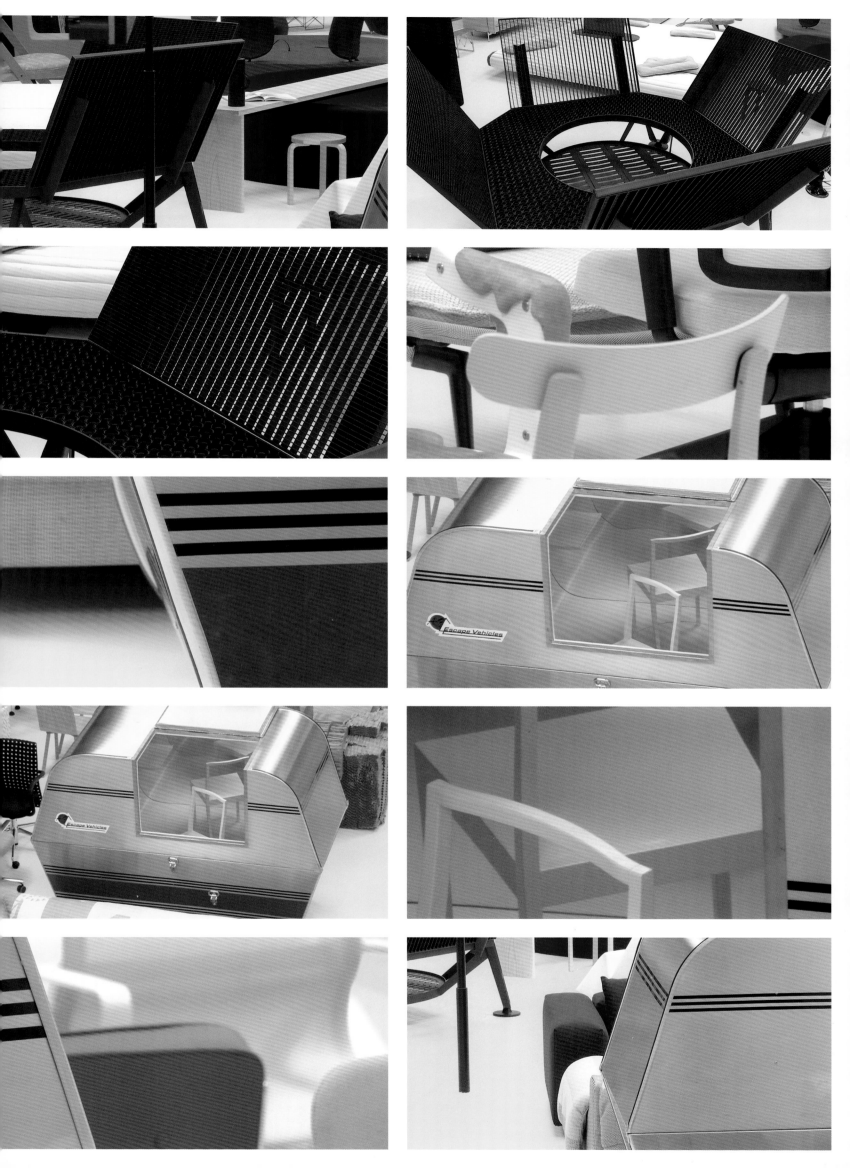

TYPECASTING
An Assembly of Iconic, Forgotten and New Vitra Characters

Edited by Robert Stadler

**Vitra
Design
Museum**

The object and its digital depiction have become an inseparable entity. The exhibition installation for Typecasting reflects that by staging the physical objects next to their live filmed video footage. This footage can be seen as both less and more than the real thing.

Robert Stadler

Staging

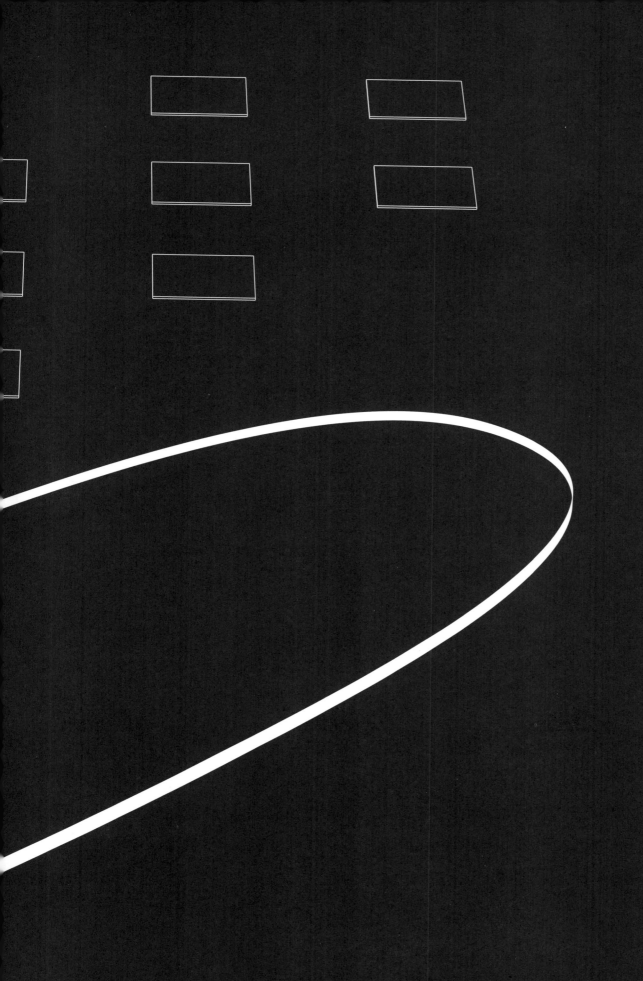

The 200 objects are displayed on a 450 m² platform. Sixteen LED panels homogeneously illuminate the scene.

Broadcasting

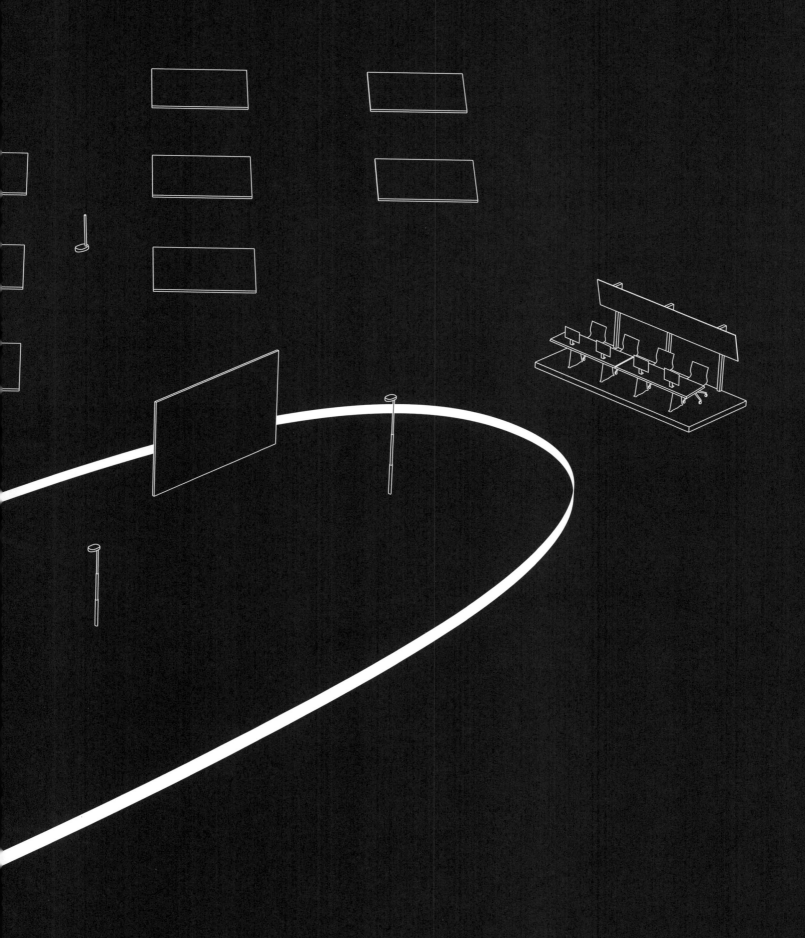

Four cameramen working from a video control station next to the stage direct six cameras. The video footage is continuously broadcast in real-time on three large LED walls.

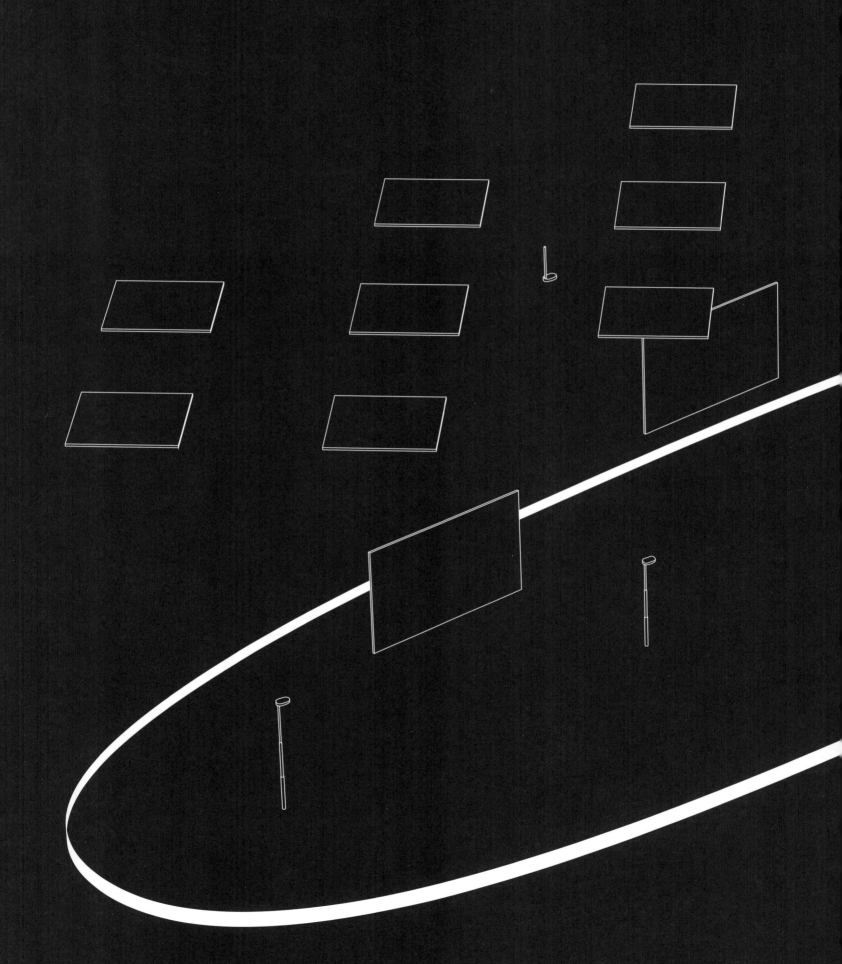

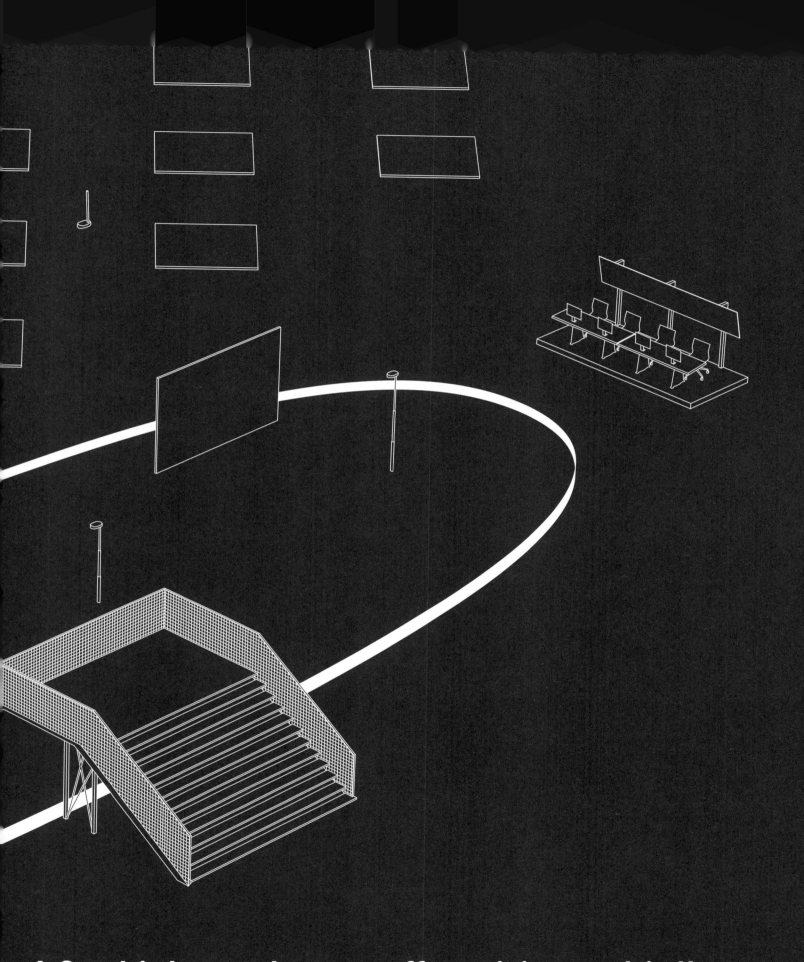

A 3m-high watchtower offers visitors a bird's-eye view in addition to the regular perspective obtained when walking around the platform.

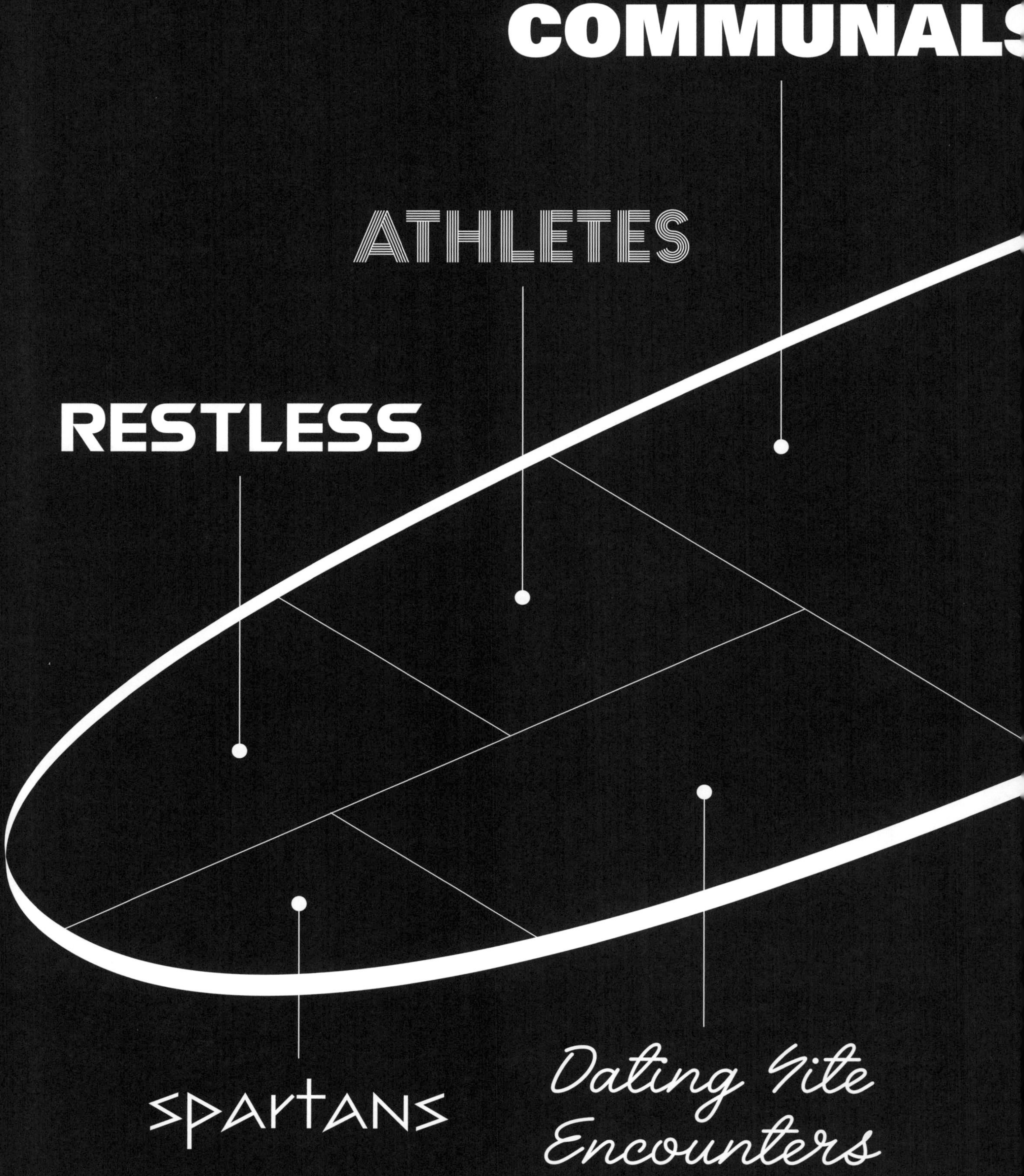

COMMUNALS

ATHLETES

RESTLESS

SPARTANS

Dating Site
Encounters

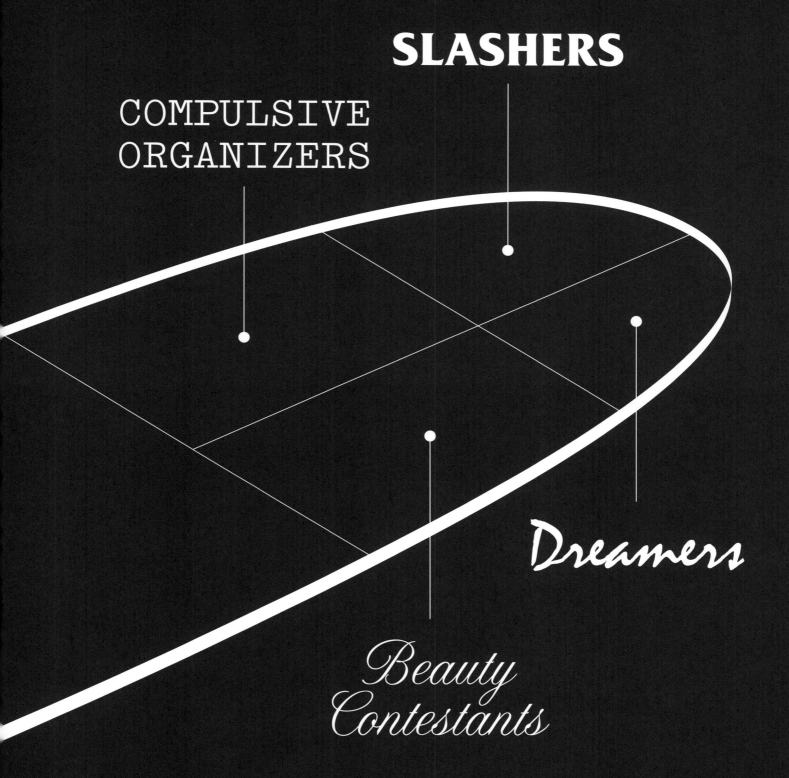

SLASHERS

COMPULSIVE ORGANIZERS

Dreamers

Beauty Contestants

The 200 objects are organised in nine different communities on the platform.

Communities

COMM

UNALS

COMMUNALS

Community profile
Living and working space is increasingly becoming rare and precious. Moreover, we often feel isolated in big cities and therefore enjoy sharing and communicating with others. Nevertheless, we experience a constant need to affirm our individuality.

Object characteristics
The shapes, materials, geometry or configurability of these objects and design studies invite people to gather.

Representative
Living Tower, Verner Panton, 1969. Vitra Production
The Living Tower is as much a sculpture as a functional piece of furniture. It is also one of the rare examples of vertical living that made it into serial production, offering both individual intimacy and communal space.

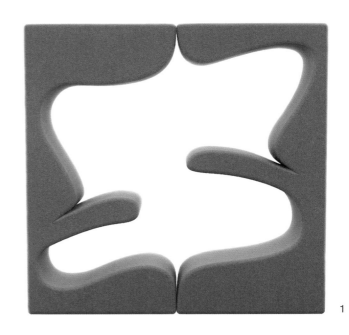

1

2

3

4

5

6

7

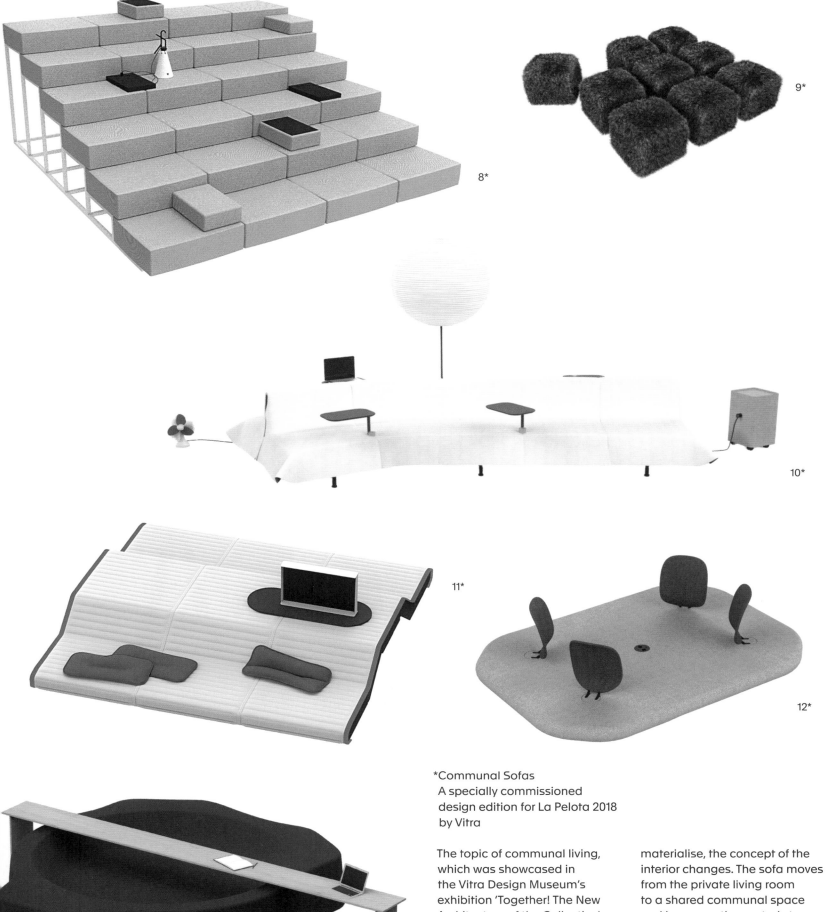

8*

9*

10*

11*

12*

13*

*Communal Sofas
A specially commissioned
design edition for La Pelota 2018
by Vitra

The topic of communal living, which was showcased in the Vitra Design Museum's exhibition 'Together! The New Architecture of the Collective', is featured in the category entitled *Communals* as the centrepiece of the installation. The traditional family apartment is losing its relevance for a growing number of urban dwellers, leading to the development of new models for communal living. As new needs materialise, the concept of the interior changes. The sofa moves from the private living room to a shared communal space and becomes the central stage for living and working together. This transfer alters its character. Ronan and Erwan Bouroullec, Konstantin Grcic, Edward Barber and Jay Osgerby, Robert Stadler, and Commonplace Studio are debuting their designs for the new typology of the 'Communal Sofa'.

COMPU
ORGAN

LSIVE
IZERS

COMPULSIVE ORGANIZERS

Community profile
The ongoing accumulation of things and data almost obliges us to become *Compulsive Organizers*. Continuously and meticulously classifying things starting from the files in our computers, has become a must for functioning in this society.

Object characteristics
Some objects, like stacking chairs, are designed to organise themselves. Others, such as drawers or hooks, help us to organise our things. And even a clock can, of course, be seen as an organisational tool.

Representative
Secretary 'Donau', Ettore Sottsass, 1990. Vitra Design Museum Collection
This secretary bears witness to pre-digital times, when we were used to organise various physical objects in order to create a personalised micro-world. Today this private, customised storage space or micro-architecture is located in our phones and computers.

1

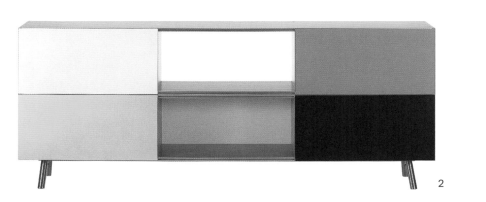
2

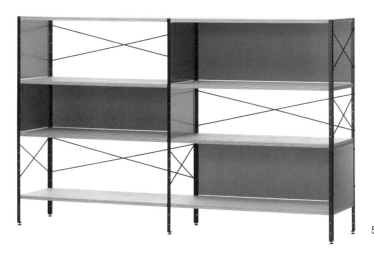
3

4

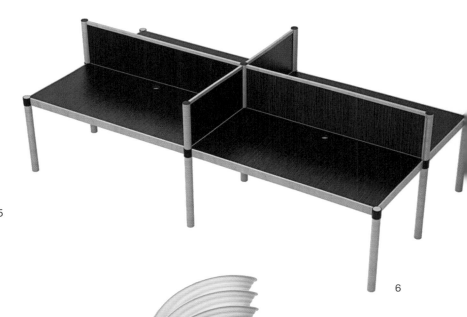
5

6

7

8

9

10

11

12

13

14

15

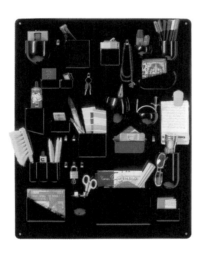

16

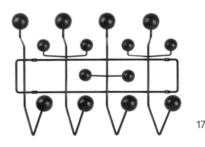

17

18

19

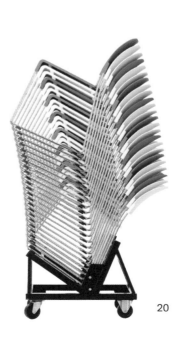

20

SLAS

HERS

SLASHERS

Community profile
Disorientation and economic instability make the Slashers assume multiple, often diverging jobs and activities, for example: designer/cupcake caterer/Uber driver. Today's infinitely available apps facilitate this trend implying nearly constant availability.

Object characteristics
Series of objects where each appears different due to a change of material or variations in shape. Today's technologies allow more and more freedom to switch materials within the same form.

Representative
Chairs, Naoto Fukasawa, 2007. Vitra Edition
This series of chairs is emblematic for the Slasher profile. By producing the same form in various materials, Fukasawa demonstrates how it is becoming increasingly easy to design a shape and then freely choose the material for it or have it made–as opposed to the past, when an object's final form was dictated to a much greater degree by the available material.

1

2

7

3

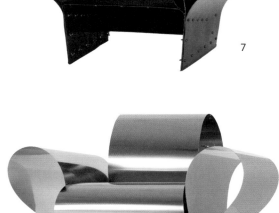
4

8

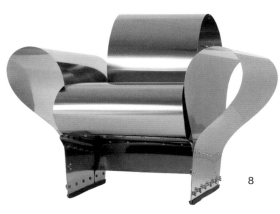
5

6

9

10

11

12

13

14

15

16

19

17

18

23

20

24

21

22

25

Drea

mers

Dreamers

Community profile

The *Dreamers* feel a strong desire to evade our hyperrational urban life by retreating into imaginary worlds. Surrounding themselves with comforting objects augments their feeling of escapism mood.

Object characteristics

This group comprises mostly smaller objects that quote or refer to nature. They are sometimes made of materials that are unusual in the design world. Not being exactly pragmatic in terms of function or appearance, their primary role is to enchant the user.

Representative

Akari BB3-33S, Isamu Noguchi, 1951. Vitra Production
Noguchi made a dream come true with his Akari light sculptures by combining materials from traditional handicraft with serial production methods. The result is a poetic object that also brilliantly fulfils a precise practical function.

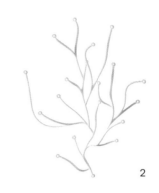

1

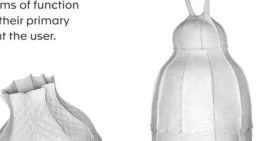

2

3

4

5

6

7

8

9

10

11

12

13

14

15

16

17

18

19

20

21

22

23

24

Bea

Conte

auty

stants

Beauty Contestants

1

Community profile

The representation of the human body and therefore its perception tends towards an increasingly fluid identity. Fluidity became a key notion for gender, digital image editing and the very community belongings we are discussing here. However, among all other qualities, this community's members share the common trait of flaunting their looks.

Object characteristics

Objects with fluid lines and strongly recognisable, sometimes anthropomorphic silhouettes. It appears that such designs were mostly produced in the 1960s and '70s.

Representative

622 NA, Charles & Ray Eames, 1959-61. Vitra Design Museum Collection

Eames chairs are champions, and their multiple qualities explain their presence in several different communities within this exhibition. Here the impeccable, sensually shaped shell makes the chair a promising favourite for the beauty contest.

2

3

4

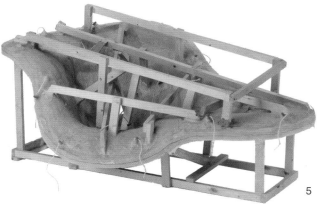

5

6

7

8

9

10

11

12

13

14

15

Datin
Encou

g Site

nters

Dating Site Encounters

Community profile

Today all kinds of people surf on dating websites hoping to find the right partner, based on presumed affinities. Algorithms 'help' to connect matching profiles, but sometimes the surprise is big when people actually meet.

Object characteristics

By arranging all objects in this community as pairs, the identity of each individual object is enhanced. Some are perfectly matched in terms of aesthetics and functions. Others share certain details or features, while further pairings represent an absolute clash.

Representatives

Soft Geometric Chair, Scott Burton, 1980. Vitra Edition_ Polder Sofa, Hella Jongerius, 2015. Vitra Production
This couple shows the fine line between art and design. Whereas Burton's Geometric Chair is almost unrecognisable as a chair, Jongerius' sofa is clearly a sofa. And yet both objects are composed following a similar logic namely by stacking geometric volumes.

1

2

3

4

5

6

7

8

9

10

11

12

13

14

15

16

17

18

19

20

21

22

23

24

25

26

27

28

29

30

31

32

33

34

35

36

37

38

39

40

SPAR

tANS

spartans

Community profile
Choosing to live with the minimum is linked to a critical view of overconsumption.

Object characteristics
These objects discard all extraneous elements sometimes to the extreme. They thereby question the minimum requirements for a piece of furniture.

Representative
MVS Chaise, Maarten Van Severen, 2000. Vitra Production
Something seems to be missing here. And yet the 'missing' length of the foot actually adds something. It allows the user to switch between two–more or less reclined–positions.

1

2

3

4

5

6

7

8

9

10

REST

LESS

RESTLESS

Community profile

Movement implies a constant change of focus and perspective. We are physically more mobile than ever before, and at the same time paradoxically many of our 'travels' are experienced virtually on the screen.

Object characteristics

These objects that can either move in some way and/or encourage the user to move–as we recognise today that a static posture not only slows down our creativity but even harms our health.

Representative

CDS, Antonio Citterio, 2016. Vitra Production
This table both moves and makes us move. The electrically adjustable table top promotes varying work postures, in contrast to the conventional stationary office table or desk.

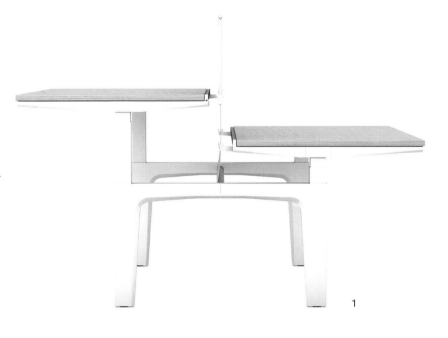

1

2

3

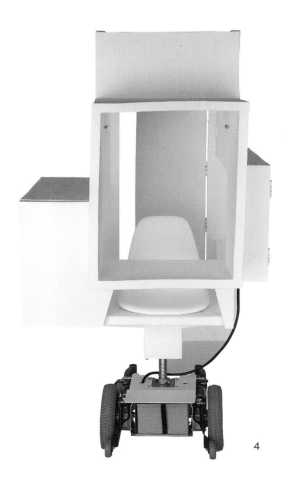

4

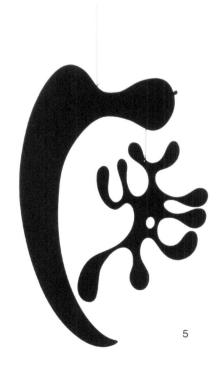

5

6

7

8

9

10

11

12

13

14

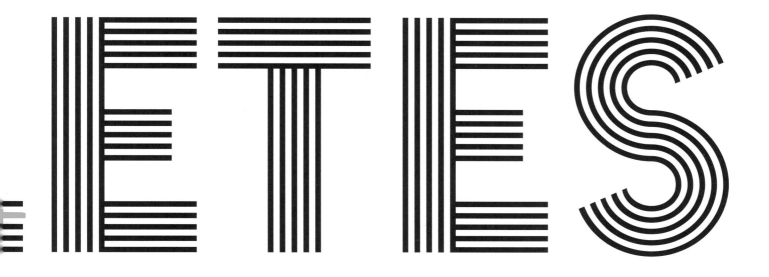

ATHLETES

Community profile
Exercise is a means of testing one's limits. The digital age, with its hyperrealistic 3D game animations, goes hand in hand with the increasing radicality of extreme sports.

Object characteristics
Various structural elements of these objects not only provide the necessary strength but are also treated here as aesthetic features.

Representative
Ypsilon, Mario & Claudio Bellini, 1998/2000. Vitra Production
Ypsilon is a typical representative of what were once called 'office machines'. Adjustment features–based on regulatory standards–and structural strength are celebrated here almost to excess.

1

2

3

4

5

6

7

8

9

10

12

11

13

15

14

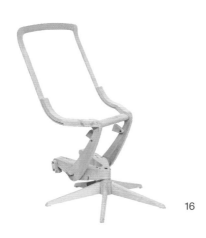

16

17

COMMUNALS

1 Living Tower, Verner Panton, 1969. Vitra Production
2 Tabula Rasa, Ginbande (Achim Heine, Uwe Fischer), 1987. Vitra Edition
3 Joyn, Ronan & Erwan Bouroullec, 2002. Vitra Production
4 Chair/Chair, Richard Artschwager, 1987. Vitra Edition
5 Social Sculpture, Studio Makkink & Bey (Jurgen Bey & Bruno Vermeersch), 2007. Vitra Design Museum Collection
6 Alcove Sofa, Ronan & Erwan Bouroullec, 2006. Vitra Production
7 Landen, Konstantin Grcic, 2007. Vitra Edition
8 SCALA, Konstantin Grcic, 2018. Prototype
9 Commonplace Ottomans, Commonplace Studio, 2018. Prototype
10 Social Docking Station, Edward Barber & Jay Osgerby, 2018. Prototype
11 Platform Sofa, Ronan & Erwan Bouroullec, 2018. Prototype
12 Hybrid, Robert Stadler, 2018. Prototype
13 Lake, Ronan & Erwan Bouroullec, 2018. Prototype

COMPULSIVE ORGANIZERS

1 Secretary Prototype, Ettore Sottsass, 1991. Vitra Design Museum Collection
2 Kast, Maarten Van Severen, 2005. Vitra Production
3 O-Tidy, Michel Charlot, 2016. Vitra Production
4 S-Tidy, Michel Charlot, 2016. Vitra Production
5 ESU Eames Storage Unit, Charles & Ray Eames, 1949. Vitra Production
6 Cyl Table, Ronan & Erwan Bouroullec, 2016. Vitra Production
7 Marshmallow Sofa, George Nelson, 1956. Vitra Production/Special
8 Tom Vac (Domus Totem), Ron Arad, 1997. Vitra Design Museum Collection
9 DSS-N, Charles & Ray Eames, 1950. Vitra Production
10 Home Desk, George Nelson, 1958. Vitra Production
11 Citizen Office Cabinet, Ettore Sottsass, 1991–93. Vitra Design Museum Collection
12 Eye Clock, George Nelson, 1948-1960. Vitra Production
13 Environmental Enrichment Panel–Geometry, Alexander Girard, 1971. Vitra Production
14 Schizzo, Ron Arad, 1989. Vitra Edition
15 Citizen Office Chair Prototype, Ettore Sottsass, 1991–93. Vitra Design Museum Collection
16 Uten.Silo I, Dorothee Becker, 1969. Vitra Production
17 Hang it all, Charles & Ray Eames, 1953. Vitra Production
18 Landi Chair, Hans Coray, 1938. Vitra Production
19 Invisible, Arik Levy, 2007. Vitra Production
20 SIM on SIM stacking dolley, Jasper Morrison, 1999. Vitra Production

SLASHERS

1 Chair (Acrylic), Naoto Fukasawa, 2007. Vitra Edition
2 Chair (Wicker), Naoto Fukasawa, 2007. Vitra Edition
3 Chair (Rimowa/Alu), Naoto Fukasawa, 2007. Vitra Edition
4 Chair (Straw), Naoto Fukasawa, 2007. Vitra Edition
5 Chair (Felt), Naoto Fukasawa, 2007. Vitra Edition
6 Chair (Polyurethane), Naoto Fukasawa, 2007. Vitra Edition
7 Bad Tempered Chair, Ron Arad, 2002. Vitra Edition
8 Well Tempered Chair, Ron Arad, 1986/87. Vitra Edition
9 Standard SP, Jean Prouvé, 1934/1950. Vitra Production
10 Standard, Jean Prouvé, 1934/1950. Vitra Production
11 No. 305, Standard Chair, Jean Prouvé, 1953. Vitra Design Museum Collection
12 Panton Chair Classic, Verner Panton, 1959/1960. Vitra Production
13 Panton Chair, Verner Panton, 1999. Vitra Production
14 Panton Chair, Verner Panton. Vitra Design Museum Collection
15 Panton Chair, Verner Panton, 1980. Vitra Design Museum Collection
16 Panton Chrome, Verner Panton, 1959/60. Vitra Production
17 Belleville Armchair Wood, Ronan & Erwan Bouroullec, 2015. Vitra Production
18 Belleville Armchair Fabric, Ronan & Erwan Bouroullec, 2015. Vitra Production
19 Leather Side Table, Ronan & Erwan Bouroullec, 2014. Vitra Production
20 Wooden Side Table, Ronan & Erwan Bouroullec, 2015. Vitra Production
21 Metal Side Table, Ronan & Erwan Bouroullec, 2004. Vitra Production
22 The Sister, Denis Santachiara, 1986/87. Vitra Edition
23 Cork Family Model A, Jasper Morrison, 2004. Vitra Production
24 Cork Family Model B, Jasper Morrison, 2004. Vitra Production
25 Cork Family Model C, Jasper Morrison, 2004. Vitra Production

Dreamers

1 Akari BB3-33S, Isamu Noguchi, 1951. Vitra Production
2 Algues, Ronan & Erwan Bouroullec, 2004. Vitra Production
3 Eames Whale, Charles & Ray Eames. Prototype
4 Office Pets, Hella Jongerius, 2007. Vitra Edition
5 Environmental Enrichment Panel–Four Leaf Clover, Alexander Girard, 1971, Vitra Production
6 Wooden Doll No.3, No.4, No. 9, Alexander Girard, 1952. Prototypes
7 Eames House Bird, Charles & Ray Eames. Vitra Production
8 L'Oiseau, Ronan & Erwan Bouroullec, 2011. Vitra Production
9 Metal Wall Relief Sun, Alexander Girard, 1966. Vitra Production
10 Bear, Front, 2018. Prototype
11 Cat, Front, 2018. Prototype
12 Birds, Front, 2018. Prototype
13 Sphere Table, Hella Jongerius, 2012. Vitra Production
14 Vegetal, Ronan & Erwan Bouroullec, 2008. Vitra Production
15 Workbay, Ronan & Erwan Bouroullec, 2006. Vitra Production
16 Butterfly Stool, Sori Yanagi, 1954. Vitra Production
17 W.W. Stool, Phillippe Starck, 1991. Vitra Production
18 Documenta Chair, Paolo Deganello, 1987. Vitra Edition
19 Wiggle Side Chair, Frank Gehry, 1972. Vitra Edition
20 Coffee Table, Isamu Noguchi, 1972/92. Vitra Production
21 Wardrobe, Boris Sipek, 1989-91. Vitra Edition
22 DCW Plywood Group, Charles & Ray Eames, 1945/1946. Vitra Production
23 Eames Elephant, Charles & Ray Eames, 1945. Vitra Production
24 The Portable Landscape, Maria Jeglinska, 2018. Prototypes

Beauty Contestants

1 622 NA, Charles & Ray Eames, 1959-61. Vitra Design Museum Collection
2 ETR Elliptical Table, Charles & Ray Eames, 1951. Vitra Production
3 Grand Repos, Alberto Citterio, 2011. Vitra Production
4 La Chaise, Charles & Ray Eames, 1948. Vitra Production
5 La Chaise Mould, Charles & Ray Eames, 1989/90. Vitra Design Museum Collection
6 Folding Screen, Charles & Ray Eames, 1946. Vitra Production
7 Freeform Sofa, Isamu Noguchi, 1946. Vitra Production/Special
8 Coconut Chair, George Nelson, 1955. Vitra Production
9 Cone Chair, Verner Panton, 1958. Vitra Production
10 Heart Cone Chair, Verner Panton, 1958. Vitra Production
11 T-Chair, Antonio Citterio, 1994. Vitra Production
12 Organic Chair, Charles Eames & Eero Saarinen, 1940. Vitra Production
13 Amoebe, Verner Panton, 1970. Vitra Production
14 Pretzel Chair, George Nelson, 1952. Vitra Limited Edition
15 Softshell Chair, Ronan & Erwan Bouroullec, 2008. Vitra Production

Dating Site Encounters

1 Soft Geometric Chair, Scott Burton, 1980. Vitra Edition
2 Polder Sofa, Hella Jongerius, 2015. Vitra Production
3 Soft Modular Sofa, Jasper Morrison, 2016. Vitra Production
4 Vlinder, Hella Jongerius, 2018. Prototype
5 Lounge Chair & Ottoman, Charles & Ray Eames, 1956. Vitra Production
6 Cité, Jean Prouvé, 1930. Vitra Production
7 Alu Chair 108, Charles & Ray Eames, 1958. Vitra Production
8 Greene Street Chair, Gaetano Pesce, 1984/86. Vitra Edition
9 Hocker, Herzog & De Meuron, 2005. Vitra Production
10 Elephant Stool, Sori Yanagi, 1954. Vitra Production

11 Prismatic Table, Isamu Noguchi, 1957. Vitra Production
12 Trienna Table, Ilmari Tapiovaara, 1954. Artek Production
13 ID Trim, Antonio Citterio, 2010. Vitra Production
14 Lobby Chair ES 104, Charles & Ray Eames, 1960. Vitra Production
15 AC1, Antonio Citterio, 1988. Vitra Product Archive
16 Pacific Chair, Edward Barber & Jay Osgerby, 2016. Vitra Production
17 .03 non-stacking, Maarten Van Severen, 1999. Vitra Production
18 .03 stacking, Maarten Van Severen, 1999. Vitra Production
19 How High The Moon, Shiro Kuramata, 1986. Vitra Edition
20 Grandpa Chair, Frank Gehry, 1987. Vitra Edition
21 Picnic Double/High Chair (Herman Miller), Charles & Ray Eames, 1950-55. Vitra Design Museum Collection
22 Lantern, Ronan & Erwan Bouroullec, 2005. Vitra Design Museum Collection
23 Santachair, Denis Santachiara, 1998. Vitra Production
24 Super Fold Table, Jasper Morrison, 2014. Vitra Production
25 AM Chair, Alberto Meda, 2016. Vitra Production
26 Slow Chair, Ronan & Erwan Bouroullec, 2006. Vitra Production
27 Vitramat, Wolfgang Müller-Deisig, 1976. Vitra Product Archive
28 HAL Armchair Studio, Jasper Morrison, 2014. Vitra Production
29 Teodora, Ettore Sottsass, 1986/87. Vitra Edition
30 Louis 20, Phillippe Starck, 1991. Vitra Production
31 .04, Maarten Van Severen, 2000. Vitra Production
32 Figura, Mario Bellini & Dieter Thiel, 1994. Vitra Product Archive
33 New Order, Jerszy Seymour, 2007. Vitra Edition
34 All Plastic Chair, Jasper Morrison, 2016. Vitra Production
35 Jill, Alfredo Häberli, 2011. Vitra Production
36 HAL Ply Wood, Jasper Morrison, 2012. Vitra Production
37 Physix, Alberto Meda, 2012. Vitra Production
38 Cork Chair, Jasper Morrison, 2008. Vitra Edition
39 Loudspeaker, Charles & Ray Eames, 1957. Vitra Design Museum Collection
40 A-Z Vehicle, Andrea Zittel, 1996. Vitra Design Museum Collection

SPARTANS

1 MVS Chaise, Maarten Van Severen, 2000. Vitra Production
2 Nelson Perch, George Nelson, 1964. Vitra Production
3 Hommage à Verner Panton, A Son of Panton Chair, Jasper Morrison, 1989/90. Vitra Design Museum Collection
4 Ply-Chair, Jasper Morrison, 1989. Vitra Edition
5 Minimum Chair, Charles & Ray Eames, 1948. Prototype
6 Potence, Jean Prouvé, 1950. Vitra Production
7 LC93B, Lage Stoel, Maarten Van Severen, 1993. Vitra Design Museum Collection
8 NesTable, Jasper Morrison, 2007. Vitra Production
9 DTM-2 Foldable Table, Charles & Ray Eames, 1947. Vitra Design Museum Collection
10 Hocker, Ginbande (Achim Heine, Uwe Fischer), 1989. Vitra Edition

RESTLESS

1 CDS, Antonio Citterio, 2016. Vitra Production
2 Balancing Tools (Scale Model), Claes Oldenburg & Coosje van Bruggen, 1984. Vitra Design Museum Collection
3 Hack, Konstantin Grcic, 2016. Vitra Production
4 Slow Car, Jurgen Bey, 2007. Vitra Edition
5 Plywood Mobile Model A, Charles & Ray Eames, 1941. Vitra Production/Special
6 Tip Ton, Edward Barber & Jay Osgerby, 2011. Vitra Production
7 Waver, Konstantin Grcic, 2011. Vitra Production
8 Visaroll 2, Antonio Citterio, 2006. Vitra Production
9 RAR Eames Plastic Chair, Charles & Ray Eames, 1950. Vitra Production
10 Citizen Office Rocking Chair Prototype, Michele De Lucchi, 1991–93. Vitra Design Museum Collection
11 Stool-Tool, Konstantin Grcic, 2016. Vitra Production
12 Caddy, Christoph Ingenhoven, 2008. Vitra Production
13 UN Lounge Chair, Hella Jongerius, 2013. Vitra Production/Special
14 es-Screen, Alberto Meda, 2007. Vitra Edition

ATHLETES

1 Ypsilon, Mario & Claudio Bellini, 1998/2000. Vitra Production
2 EM Table, Jean Prouvé, 1950. Vitra Production
3 Mesa, Zaha Hadid, 2007. Vitra Edition
4 LTR Occasional Table, Charles & Ray Eames, 1950. Vitra Production
5 Meda Gate, Alberto Meda, 2011. Vitra Production
6 Dining Table, Isamu Noguchi, 1954/55. Vitra Production
7 EFC Eames Fiberglass Chair, Charles & Ray Eames, 1950. Vitra Production
8 DKW-2 Wire Chair, Charles & Ray Eames, 1951. Vitra Production
9 Light Standing Fixture, Frank Gehry, 1993. Vitra Design Museum Collection
10 Leg Splint, Charles & Ray Eames, 1941/42. Vitra Product Archive
11 Allstar, Konstantin Grcic, 2014. Vitra Production
12 Hexagonal Table, Alexander Girard, 1967. Vitra Production
13 Click!, Alberto Meda, 2006. Vitra Production
14 AC5 Swift, Antonio Citterio, 2017. Vitra Production
15 Vodöl, Coop Himmelblau, 1989. Vitra Edition
16 Ergonomic Chair Prototype, Vitra Product Archive
17 Ergonomic Chair Prototype. Vitra Product Archive

Designer Panels

Designer Panels

Round Table moderated by Jan Boelen

Mon Apr 16, 2018

**Edward Barber
Erwan Bouroullec
Konstantin Grcic
Rolf Fehlbaum
Hella Jongerius
Maria Jeglinska
Sofia Lagerkvist
Anna Lindgren
Chrissie Muhr
Robert Stadler
Jon Stam**

Jan Boelen

Typecasting: When objects start to function as actors in different ways. The world is a stage in itself and the objects are part of this super-inspiring environment, especially in today's age of self-staging, of the selfie, the hashtag and the shelfie, where people actually become part of their very environment. The shelfie is a brand of clothes that is completely made for the selfie. There's no back—and this was exactly what I was asking Rolf (Fehlbaum) this morning. When will this chair be done with the back for self-staging? I would like to start with the exhibition and what you could call *Typecasting*. The objects are categorised. It's as if somebody else has almost put a stamp on them and said this is now—you. Like Maria, from now on you are a *Dreamer*. But then, all of you are also staging your work in a very particular way. You create a narrative and present it in a sort of exhibition. Very strict, like Hella or Konstantin, when you organise the objects in the photographs, so even analysing the photographs is like an issue itself. A large part of your work is not only the object but exhibition design and staging per se. And all these worlds come together if I look at Front. From the beginning, you were playing with this real/unreal, virtual/materialised world, as a continuous dialogue. Jon, who was a student of mine, was always toying with the virtual and the real, bringing the cloud and the object together, and then animating it. Every time I saw him in recent years, he was focussing on how the algorithm is also a certain philosophy. So here we are on this stage, in this television studio, you could say, or in this imaginary Instagram, because that is what will happen now: everybody will start making pictures. I find all this staging very fascinating, but also problematic because it's not about the object itself anymore, but about the message we want to convey: the media is taking over. It's no longer about design anymore, the design is secondary.

Rolf Fehlbaum

If you look at Charles Eames's photography, you see what was possibly the first consistent professional staging in the world of design. Through Billy Wilder, Charles was acquainted with Hollywood and understood the power of the image. So products, the office, and Charles and Ray were pictured in a thoroughly curated way. So it's not a completely new phenomenon.

Hella Jongerius

I also believe, like ten years ago, we were all staged in magazines. And now the platform is democratic, so we can all stage ourselves. There's no hierarchy; anybody can do whatever staging they like. And you could say that furniture becomes more of an accessory, by virtue of being multiplied by mass industry. But to be honest, I don't see so much of a difference in comparison to the situation before.

Jan Boelen
I see a difference, if I look at how objects become animated and start to move. Robots and things. That is because the object itself starts to resemble technology and also interacts with the technology. This is not neutral, and the animation starts to surround us.

Robert Stadler
And so does the staging. OK, staging is not new, but as we know, nothing ever is. The self-staging and also the importance of how to communicate ideas or objects has, of course, always existed. But it's interesting to see that it was not always motivated by the same ideas. For example, in the 1960s they were very good at communicating ideas with an ideology. There was a desire for a rupture with certain ideas that had gone before. But is this still happening? Is any kind of idea still out there? Or is it staging, or self-staging for the sake of self-staging? Or the image for the sake of the image? I think there is a different mood today with digital media and the extreme dissemination of images. Also I'm not so sure about the democratic aspect you mentioned, Hella. Because when you have the power to have many followers, it kind of kills the ones who have far fewer. That's how today's big corporations massively take over this space. And this is not exactly democratic.

Edward Barber
But then it's up to you though, isn't it? Still, to get followers on Instagram is a full-time job.

Robert Stadler
That's the point, it's a full-time job. And you can only efficiently do it if you have the facilities, the staff, and the means to do so.

Konstantin Grcic
I think what really changes starts as early as when you have 100 followers. And that's when you start thinking about your followers, and you create the image for the followers, rather than for yourself…

Jan Boelen
300 followers…

Konstantin Grcic
Exactly. I do think that the images, specifically the photographic images, are very important. I learned this thanks to a close friend who is a photographer. Together we developed ideas for photographs, and they were a testing ground for myself, first of all. A kind of visual groundwork in communication. We were interested in testing why a particular image would start to flip, or even fail to transmit what we wanted it to transmit. The purpose of these images was not to please others or make them follow us. I can't imagine myself doing that quality of imagery thinking about 1,000 followers, because that would kind of place me in the service of those followers. And I don't believe anyone who has that many followers is as radical and self-driven as we all are when we're working without a consciousness of the public reception. We do it for other reasons, primarily for ourselves as part of our own research.

Jan Boelen
The first pictures that I remember are the Authentics objects in the public space and nature. They kind of decontextualised the objects from where they should belong in order to understand them better. How they function, how they react…

Rolf Fehlbaum
Do you think that changes the work of the designer? I mean, everybody wants to do work that will please somebody, and everybody wants to do work that will sell eventually. Will it change the designers' job if they start wondering first how it will look in an image?

Konstantin Grcic
I think it encourages us to be even more radical. Images don't really hurt anyone, which means that you can push them quite far. In architecture it has become an interesting phenomenon how highly realistic renderings are posted on certain Internet platforms to get projects published at a very early stage. A certain type of architecture seems to be designed with only that iconic image in mind. I had a memorable experience with the Phaeno museum in Wolfsburg, by Zaha Hadid. A picture in a newspaper made me go and see it. In that particular photograph–or was it a rendering–the building looked absolutely stunning. But when I went there I arrived from the rear side of the building, which seemed so inferior in comparison. All that seemed to matter was the one perspective, the beauty shot.

Hella Jongerius
There's a name for that: they call it the 'money shot'. They only design the building for that specific shot. And you could say that's what you lose if you only work for a photograph, you lose the optical and haptic feeling of a product. That's a crucial element. And also, it's theatre if the design is just for the photo. If functionality is not important. Or if it's only visual functionality.

Edward Barber
If you look around the fair every year, a vast majority of the pieces that are put out are purely about photography, about that one image.

Hella Jongerius
Yes, but the question is, is that quality or is that our profession?

Konstantin Grcic

And most of the time they are actually renderings done by the designers. Because the companies are never ready with the product… Which makes it all the more absurd.

Robert Stadler

So there's a question that comes up. Most of us here, being non-digital natives, have grown up with a certain definition of 'good design', meaning how things should be done in a serious way, taking all aspects that make a good product into account. One of those aspects is the importance of the object's experience in terms of its haptic qualities–or in architecture, where it is even more complex because there the experience of movement in space is involved. So what is happening to this definition in the digital age? It seems it is shifting. Taking it one step further, we could ask if we actually continue to need to experience the real thing? Or is this criteria from the past? Is the image the final product?

Edward Barber

If we judge it in terms of the international scope–you know, if a chair is launched this year, all the people will see that image. But only five or ten percent might ever see it in real life, and maybe one percent or less will actually own it. So the image is incredibly important.

Robert Stadler

So it actually is about the consumption of the image, more than the consumption of the product.

Jon Stam

For the designer, however, the image can also create some distance when you start to question your choices. I find it really hard to say that you're making the product only for the image. When you're making images you can actually double-check or question whether your choices are the right ones.

Jan Boelen

But I also think it's important that images are made by designers–take Konstantin's 'Panorama', for example. Or the work you made, Anna, whereby the performance is also showing a possibility. The designer has the potential to create these images, so it's nice to be critiquing, but we also have the power to make these images.

Anna Lindgren

We made a computer game back in 2003, and we were having the same discussion we are having right now. All the things that are shown by all these companies end up as press images, and perhaps 50 per cent is actually produced in the end. And we said, what other opportunities are there? If we produce something

directly from an image, what can it do? And we made things in rooms that didn't have any gravity, so they were flying. Or things were divided and put together again in a new way. New technology can always be something that gives a new perspective as well.

Robert Stadler
Whenever there's a new trend, there is always luckily a contrary reaction from people. The current interest in craftsmanship, for example, is probably a reaction to the omnipresence of digital devices. The sleeker things become, the more we want to see the opposite, like imperfection and human intervention. Things never just go in one direction.

Jan Boelen
Maria, does that work for you?

Maria Jeglinska
I think so, yes. It has its pros and cons, but it's definitely a good platform to get your work out there. I do Instagram or Wave, and we've been doing books, which you can then feed back into the digital world. Also it's a great tool for just looking at everything that's happening. An observation point, where to go, what to do.

Robert Stadler
Has your Instagram presence ever resulted in a job?

Maria Jeglinska
No, no, no.

Chrissie Muhr
But you can see that young designers and architects no longer have a website. They use Instagram instead, because it's really direct. Not only can you show and file projects, you can also show the whole process. You make images of the production process or offer insights into your studio practice.

Jan Boelen
That's also true for you guys. You do that almost strategically.

Erwan Bouroullec
For me there is not much debate about a picture or no picture. I see it like a fight. Rolf, you've been building this company for several decades, and Vitra was not a given thing 30 or 40 years ago. You had to do anything you could to exist, survive, make it grow. I think design as we envision it is a very important practice, so we should do whatever we can do to make it succeed. Now to question the role of the image, and if the role of the image could have some consequences for product design itself–perhaps. But if you see it more as a fight, it is a strength you should never forget.

So yes, it's definitely strategic–every image we make, we carefully value what it is, when, for whom, it's all very precise ...

Jan Boelen
Like snipers. But when you look at the *Communals*, one part of this exhibition, a new kind of typology is emerging.

Erwan Bouroullec
Yes, and I didn't want to be cynical. It's just that we often don't make any changes, but we are providing novelties for the sake of novelties. I think society needs signs of change. It is not that the functionality is really needed–and anyway, there is not much typological evolution for chairs and tables. I always use this example even if it's a little bit fake: a 65-year-old guy wants to renew his restaurant. He doesn't know anything about design. But he is alive and part of the contemporary world, and he simply wants a visible sign of that. Then, and for that reason only, he chooses a so-called designer chair that expresses contemporaneity. So, somehow things are already pictures themselves. And most of the time, what a design object communicates most is its novelty, its sign of contemporariness.

Robert Stadler
I think this is true for one definition of design, but to me the great thing with design is that you can approach it and also practise it in so many ways. It's like a mirror ball where each facet reflects something different. So your example is certainly true for product and furniture design that is meant for serial production, which actually is a big and important part of this exhibition. But then there were and are other approaches in design which are just as relevant. There was Bruno Munari in the past, and there are various forms of critical design today. A lot of those works are not meant for production; they are more about the message, the content, so they aim at something different.

Erwan Bouroullec
What I wanted to say is that society simply also needs emblematic signs. If you take the Panton Chair, for example, it was an incredibly good sign. Now it is everywhere; it is exploited like a logo. It's more a picture than furniture. I know some people who have inherited a very early Panton Chair and they say: 'I have this Panton Chair from my parents.' What they are indirectly saying is: 'My parents were already into progress back in the 1960s.' And this is an important motive behind design, but we rarely acknowledge it. We never say: I'm making design as a sign.

Robert Stadler
To respond to Jan, you were referring to the *Communals*, and to the new prototypes. Design–just like fashion

and other creative fields–often acts as a kind of seismograph of our times. The zeitgeist if you like. Sometimes they just respond to trends, sometimes they try to provoke and set the tone. I think what we all tried with these new 'Communal Sofas' is to discern today's situation–which of course, again, is not new, because the communal idea existed back in the 1930s and then again in the 1960s during the hippie era. But we did it now with today's concerns and today's available technologies. All our designs have this idea of a free platform enabling a more open or fluid way to use it compared to a traditional two-seater. Some are mobile, others are not, but anyhow they create a new typology, and it's a little more than a sign in the sense of being an aesthetic comment. And maybe some of them will become a sign, but they still have somewhat deeper motivations.

Jan Boelen
Yes, and people are really on stage when using these platforms. Your Vlinder (sofa) also works in that way, Hella.

Hella Jongerius
Yes, it is a response to social changes. And that is, I believe, more than just making a sign–which in my opinion is not enough today. Maybe it is important that this is one of the layers, but I find it important that it responds to social or cultural changes, or to technology–which is difficult, because after all so much is changing in materials and technology. It's not really an active field. But for me I need more than the layer of making a sign, and for you too, I think.

Erwan Bouroullec
I didn't say that this is my objective, but often it is one way that people use design. There are just a lot of design addicts, and they show you what they own just like a collection of icons. Of course, here we are in a different story, because Vitra does very strong research on people's posture and ergonomics. The ergonomics of individuals as well as groups. And in some wonderful cases, the sign arises from its own logic and ergonomics. I always liked the Ypsilon chair. To me, this is an example of something that is a sign of its own program.

Jan Boelen
To come back to what was said before: these objects become part of a staged reality, where the objects of a company like Vitra are also used. At Airbnb, for example, you see reproduced realities that are continuously sold, and we can ask ourselves if this is an interesting evolution...

Robert Stadler
The objects become props of those realities.

Konstantin Grcic
And they change in connotation; last night you mentioned this agency where one can exchange flats…

Robert Stadler
Yes, it's a kind of high-end online platform for people working in the creative business. A so-called community… So one would expect to find lots of very special and personal interiors there, but actually most of the apartments look very much alike. With a magazine-like mix of Modernist and contemporary, you know…

Konstantin Grcic
Fifteen years ago, if you travelled and wanted to rent an apartment somewhere else and found, say, a loft-type space with an Eames Chair in the corner, you would have been super happy. Today they all have that Eames Chair in the corner. Besides that, we don't know if they're all authentic. It's an image that was still kind of amazing 15 years ago, even avant-garde. And now it's totally banal. You flip through hundreds of those and you don't go for any of them anymore.

Jan Boelen
This expression of so-called modernity and progress has become an interchangeable reality that is copy-pasted.

Konstantin Grcic
But why is this called progress? If this is avant-garde and progressive, then why is it so retro-oriented? The generation of the Panton Chair, now they made quite a radical statement by buying the chair when it came out. Why are the hundreds of Airbnb flats furnished with, you know, the…

Hella Jongerius
…the furniture of yesterday.

Edward Barber
Because it is comfortable. The average person doesn't want to be challenged renting out an apartment…

Konstantin Grcic
And why have our expectations and mentality changed so much that we have lost our courage or a sense of adventure? Why do we have to be comforted with things that are familiar?

Robert Stadler
Well, that's exactly what the exhibition also critically reflects on with the title *Typecasting*. This home exchange website I've mentioned before is directly related to this situation. It's typecast for a certain group of people. They have to be creatives in order to be accepted in the club—so somehow we are the perfect target.

Hella Jongerius
No, I think we are not.

Robert Stadler
And this is the paradox. Why not? Because we feel boxed in and we want to break out of this frame.

Rolf Fehlbaum
Here you see the success of design. I mean, when I started, design was not a mass phenomenon. It was a rather elitist issue. Only a few magazines covered it, and now there are hundreds of them. Back then, the Eameses were known primarily to architects. Now the designers are known to mainstream consumers. So isn't that the victory of design?

Robert Stadler
It's a victory, but on the other hand, it kills the adventurous discovery process because it has turned us into more passive consumers. It's much more difficult to discover something new today, because most of the time someone else has already pointed it out and often in a very professional and visible way. A few years ago I found this wonderful company in Japan that does cast-iron pans. And I paid a lot in excess baggage to take some of them home to Paris, and then at one point I went to that stupid concept store next to my place— and they were selling these very pans! I was so happy to discover them, but then…

Rolf Fehlbaum
If somebody could do something about it, it's you, the designers. And so why don't you come up with those stunning new things?

Edward Barber
To be able to do good things as a designer or an architect, you have to rely on a great client. You need to have someone who does not necessarily understand you, but allows you to dream. However, clients like that are incredibly hard to find.

Hella Jongerius
That's how I see it, too. I have now done three design shows in a museum, because I find a platform in a museum is now much more open and lets me express what I want to talk about. For me, there is more freedom there than in the industrial commercial context.

Edward Barber
The same thing happens with the clients of an interior architect. They have the same mentality as that expressed by this Airbnb kind of comfort. They still want that sort of familiarity; they don't want to alienate anyone, make them feel too cold or too this or too that.

Robert Stadler

Talking about interiors, I think the designers missed a chance in recent years, because now it's the decorators who make the decisions, and this has also become a huge business. In former times it was the architects, the great designer/architects whom we all know, who not only designed the objects and furnishings, but also the spaces. Today most of us here are focussing on the object and don't have a vision for the whole interior. And so it's the decorators who do that job.

Jan Boelen

But all the people gathered here around the table are also into exhibition design, and you yourself are also restaging and reconfiguring objects within museum displays, so you also create your own experimental playgrounds...

Robert Stadler

True, but if I think of all the design galleries that have become big, they've teamed up with interior designers. Today they are the galleries' biggest clients—it's not the collectors anymore. And those decorators, that's not us. They generally don't sell the kind of world we construct in an experimental context, such as an exhibition.

Edward Barber

I think that's even starting to move on. The decorators are now looking at the gallery pieces and saying: 'Oh, I could do that.'

Rolf Fehlbaum

So what would be a really contemporary attitude? I mean you, Konstantin, with your Chair One you created a chair that defines a period more than any other chair I can think of. You said it's a pity to look back, so how would you define a contemporary chair?

Konstantin Grcic

I think the issue is behaviour. The behaviour of a single person and also of a group of people and how they interact. That's the fodder for a lot of projects that we are all doing, and the 'Communal Sofa' is a perfect example. I imagined my sofa to be used by a group of people and also disconnected smaller groups sharing the same thing. The issue of behaviour is so fascinating, because there is never the right formula. It's a very dynamic material to work with. For me every chair poses the question: what kind of chair, for what kind of sitting, for how long, for whom, in what context and so on? Of course, what has changed from the chairs you were referring to is that today there are no dictates on how we have to sit. And it is interesting that in the office environment we don't sit on office chairs any longer. We do, but we sit on a lot of other chairs or sofas as well. It just shows how easily all of this changes. Now we think the sofa is great to work on, and in ten years' time something else will be the preferred choice.

Jan Boelen

But it is not true that it changes so easily, because Chair One took several years before it caught on.

Konstantin Grcic

For me it's also a problem, because I didn't design it to be an icon. I think it's mistaken as a very graphic, iconic chair. For me it was a chair with a very clear destination. An outdoor piece of urban furniture. It was made in the way it was made so that it wouldn't get dirty, and rain wouldn't collect on it, and it would be neither too hot in summer nor too cold in winter, and robust enough so that it couldn't be vandalized. That was my idea of the chair. Now you find it in a restaurant. And I feel for people who have to sit through a dinner on it. Because it was never intended for that.

Robert Stadler

So why and how this chair happened is actually very different from what made it successful. Again, it's the chair as a sign. It's the image.

Konstantin Grcic

The architects Herzog & de Meuron bought the chair for the café of the de Young museum in San Francisco. So again it's about the power of images. Because the museum was published a lot in architectural magazines, its blessing was bestowed on the chair. And from then on other people believed in it, like 'Ah, that chair is for real and it works.' Only then did it start to sell.

Edward Barber

To go back to ergonomics, a couple of projects we've done with Vitra have relied on studying ergonomics to actually try and find a different way of doing something. Tip Ton was the first one. It was originally designed for schools, and we worked with a university studying how people, when they sat forward, have a straighter spine and blood flow increases because you are moving. All these things. And we took it very seriously and came up with this new typology of chair for the workplace or for the school. But the reality is that at least half of the sales are usually by people for their homes, for the kitchen table.

Rolf Fehlbaum

Now what about these 'Communal Sofas'? Is that just an interesting study and tomorrow something else will come, or do you think it's something that will have an impact? Is it a new typology or is it just a fantasy? What do you think?

Robert Stadler

I think it's a phenomenon that was already there. But then these ideas keep on popping up in history, but always in a different form because tastes change, technology changes. Anyhow, I think you should tell us, especially because I remember when we had talked about the communal living idea, you said: 'Oh, these 'Communal Sofas', Verner Panton already said that the classical sofa is dead, but then look what happened…'

Rolf Fehlbaum

That's a very strange thing. When I worked with Verner Panton in the 1960s, we indeed thought classical furniture was dead. We thought we would never go back to tables and sofas, that they were over. We literally believed in 3D carpets and these total environments. And one result of the discussion was the Living Tower. And then, all of a sudden this vision disappeared. Sofas and tables returned. Back then there was also Superstudio and Archizoom and other people who wanted to change the world of interiors. There is an interest today in their work. Is that a sign of renewal? Another question we have asked ourselves in recent years was whether innovation actually happens in the office, not the home. But now with offices and homes getting closer, the home becomes a place of change again. We were doing this exhibition entitled 'Together' [at the Vitra Design Museum in 2017] and became very interested in this new world of living and working together and sharing space, tools, and furniture. So the 'Communal Sofa' became the new centrepiece of communal living, replacing the sofa of Mummy and Daddy and the TV. Is that happening just in a particular scene or will it become a new standard? I don't know, but I find it exciting to think about.

Maria Jeglinska

I think the topic of the 'Communal Sofa' is the essence of what today's space looks like. Because we will define the physical space, the walls, much more by the activities. And although they're completely different typologies, that's what I wanted to address with what I call the 'Portable Landscape': this small object with plants that you can reconfigure.

Robert Stadler

Maybe what is different today is that architects provide those open spaces where 'Communal Sofas' can finally fit in. In the 1960s, when Panton did his large furniture landscapes, they had to fit in a traditional house, which is tricky. Today there are all these big companies, real estate developers, who invest in co-working and co-living spaces. These buildings are planned with large communal spaces and very limited private spaces and bedrooms. So maybe there is a real chance today that the 'Communal Sofa' can finally exist.

Erwan Bouroullec

But the bigger change is due to mobile technology. That is one of the main factors, as now we kind of switch all the time from work to home to work to private…

Robert Stadler

Or we don't switch anymore.

Erwan Bouroullec

And so it's been totally liberating for the posture of the body. Even 15 years ago, to send an email you needed to be in front of a table because you had a deep screen and you needed to type. I see, for example, that for my daughters, the typology we have at home, our bedroom, kitchen, living room, makes no sense at all. For them, there is no location that is made for something. Maybe the thing that lasts is the bed for sleeping. For me the very best 'Communal Sofa' that was done in recent years was the SANAA building, the Rolex Center. We increasingly live in something like a jungle, because we are physically disconnected from the things around us. Our mind is somewhere and our body is somewhere else. This creates very strange situations, in which people are on the phone while crossing the street, without checking the red lights. As if the body is over-ruling the brain. It is very nice to see what is happening with the Alcove sofa. People just go there naturally. Yours, Konstantin, looks like a football stadium, but it also looks like a mountain, and I think it's ideal today because sometimes you can go up or down: it's very instinctive. And so is the Rolex Center. You just wander through and you don't know why you stop somewhere. So I think the 'Communal Sofa' is probably more about deconstruction of the pre-set signs, of typology. Another future for the 'Communal Sofa' might be something like cars, like a prefabricated cell…

Jan Boelen

Konstantin, that was an issue for you in regard to the Studiolo, this furniture piece defining an individual space. And the infrastructure can be outside and can be shared. This is a new way of living that is really popping up now. Where the cell, a fully private space, becomes the place where your identity is, and then the rest is a shared environment. This is also not new, because in the 1930s this already happened in the United States and in Russia as well.

Hella Jongerius

Let's talk about this shutting off your mind and your body as an identity of its own with its own physical intelligence. Then it also makes sense that haptics are so very important, namely that your body really feels and experiences a kind of privacy in the surface. Or a kind of texture. But then I think the skin becomes very important, and you have private textile skins that you want to have entirely for yourself, because it's also something that gets dirty. You have the feeling that if everybody is sitting on this textile you will not feel comfortable. In this regard, textile is a very important topic if we are talking about communal living.

Jan Boelen
It's also something that has existed throughout history. From carpet-making and bringing the narratives into the kilims.

Hella Jongerius
Besides textiles are also becoming so downgraded – due to the last ten years in the fashion industry with H&M and Primark, and this very shitty industry where the textile itself, as a material, has a very poor quality because it has to be very, very cheap and very rapidly produced, so there are no more interesting bindings, and it's all digitally printed. We're losing skills and we also have problems like slavery in India, and in China. Then there are these chemicals. One fourth of all the chemicals in the world are used in the textile industry. Just unbelievable.

Erwan Bouroullec
And a lot of water, too…

Hella Jongerius
A lot of water. It's so polluted. So not only are textiles a tactile topic, but also a crucial phenomenon as

an industry that we have to address, also from the social point of view. That's why I did the study on the Vlinder sofa.

Jan Boelen
So if we slowly try to wrap this up – it's really staging and choreography or movements which are continuously coming back into the discussion. Also it is very interesting how we brought in the topic of ergonomics. So maybe *Typecasting* is us acting, but does designing help manipulate the movements? And there it can become very directive, like when certain chairs move you into a certain position. Do we want this?

Erwan Bouroullec
Rolf was asking what would be a great success now. I think now the ergonomics of most chairs are very poor, and at the same time they are extremely strong social signs. What would be progress, in my view, is if it were the other way round.

Edward Barber
There is a massive trend towards sharing, like music, Airbnb, bicycles, or cars. No one really owns their things anymore. It's interesting that these 'Communal Sofas' are again about sharing. Sharing that space and interacting with other people. There are so many people in major cities around the world and if you work on your own, you don't necessarily need to rent a studio or an

office, because you can go into a hotel lobby where you have free Wi-Fi, somewhere to sit. And the hotel will welcome you because you will end up buying coffee there or maybe lunch. So that has been a massive social shift in the last five or ten years. We were talking about people being excluded because they can't afford stuff, but people can actually access more.

Konstantin Grcic
From my experience, designing for a very specific kind of situation creates something that then proves to be much more hybrid, much more flexible. We all know that as designers, trying to design 'the flexible system' is impossible: you fail.

Jon Stam
Isn't it the actual joy of seeing the appropriation of something that you've made? That someone else is taking ownership and deciding what to do–there's something beautiful about that. Whereas if you're trying to be the person who claims this appropriation of an object by designing it in different ways, you're actually ruining the magic moment when someone decides to do something different.

Erwan Bouroullec
But there is still something here you need to be careful about, namely the symbolic property of novelties. In our case, Algue is an example, which people adapt and transform, and many are the times I've seen really bad installations of it. As if people were thinking: 'This is new so I need to do something new.' So instead of making a nice, easy composition on a wall, some people place it on the ceiling in the toilet, others wrap it around the staircase handles. I always think design has a kind of excessive placebo effect. And this is important to control. People want to extract so much novelty out of things that it can get totally corrupted.

Hella Jongerius
I think it's a very good sign that there are so many open options that people can do their own thing and that you can't control it and there's imperfection and another life for your work.

Erwan Bouroullec
It just depends–you can see many working environments offering various communal situations and often, they end up with the worst. We are in an age where we value novelties above all else. So all companies want to say: 'We've been changing, we've been changing.' And sometimes they value the sign of change more than a positive building behind the change. We really should be aware of this.

Robert Stadler
I agree with Hella, and there's also something sweet about all those 'wrong' uses. We as designers have to accept that things go out in the world and then people do something with them. Otherwise, you're an artist and your artwork comes with a precise installation protocol. But if you do a product that's industrially produced and widely distributed… I had the same slightly disconcerting experience when we as RADI Designers did the electrical kitchen appliances for Moulinex. I would see our toasters and coffee machines in Airbnb homes and I sometimes was a little bit shocked at first because of the overall environment. But in the end I kind of liked the fact these objects lead their own lives. Otherwise it would be as if you were a musician getting angry if someone puts your song in a playlist where you don't like the other songs, come on…

Sofia Lagerkvist
Designers should do more studies about what happens with the products and what kind of effect they have on peoples' lives and learn from that, use it as a tool to do new things. We can be inspired by what people do and–as regards the 'Communal Sofas'–see what can actually happen with them. I'm sure they will create different settings in each place.

Talk moderated by Jan Boelen

Wed Apr 18, 2018

**Erwan Bouroullec
Maria Jeglinska
Jay Osgerby
Sofia Lagerkvist
Anna Lindgren
Robert Stadler
Jon Stam**

Jan Boelen
Welcome Ladies and Gentlemen. Welcome to Vitra at La Pelota here in Milan and welcome to joining us for this talk, or rather image-based conversation where objects function as the actors. This project was created by Robert Stadler, he's the curator of the exhibition called *Typecasting*: So what do we see Robert?

Robert Stadler
Hello. We see about 200 objects from Vitra, varying in scale, date and function. Objects from the past, the present, and also the future, as there are six new design studies which are presented here for the first time. We also see three large LED screens displaying videos of the exhibited objects so we perceive the objects and their images simultaneously. As for the title, *Typecasting* is a term used in cinema and also theatre when an actor is repeatedly cast for similar stereotypical roles, such as the villain, the vamp, the action hero or the beauty. As you already said, in this exhibition the furniture is presented as characters. Those characters are grouped in nine different communities amongst which are the *Compulsive Organizers*, the *Beauty Contestants*, the *Communals*, etc. So the idea was to focus not only on the practical or ergonomic aspect of design, but also its social role. My main concern was that the exhibition should be as much about furniture as about us.

Jan Boelen
Then maybe it's good to start to talk a little bit about what we see here? Erwan, what is your part in the *Communals*?

Erwan Bouroullec
I think the first thing that we see is a part of the Vitra testimony and legacy on a communal surface, of which we are part. However, for me the fundamental aspect is to see all these things together. It's very important that design is made for people in movement. An everyday movement, but also a social movement …

Jan Boelen
What we see here appears like a stage made for a television studio. And the objects are basically presented against a background for Photoshop, and they are like super instagrammable and suddenly become icons.

Erwan Bouroullec
Honestly, I don't think that is instagrammable. Only if you find it sufficient to get just one global image about it. What is very interesting in this show is to see yourself as you go along so many different paths. So many different things and, well, the world is a little bit more complex than expected. Somehow I live in a time in which I feel less and less at ease. To see that we produce more and more things for lives that look so leisurely.

So here we see something else, and I think Robert created a very interesting picture of Vitra, but there is also something rough. It's a little bit electric, not very gentle. And that's very nice. Life is more complicated than what we produce.

Jan Boelen
The world is a stage. As part of Front, Sofia and Anna, what do we see from you here? What is on the stage? What kind of world are you showing here?

Anna Lindgren
This is the first project that we have shared with Vitra and it's been a fantastic collaboration. We're showing a series of animals that are asleep. They are accessories, but they hope they will move into people's homes and bring with them an element of nature, calmness and companionship. We are part of the *Dreamers* section.

Jan Boelen
OK. We'll come back to that later. Maria, your work is also over there…

Maria Jeglinska
Yes, I'm right next to Front so I'm also part of the *Dreamers* group. I'm presenting a project called 'The Portable Landscape' which addresses several issues I observed relating to the fact that our lives have become so complex with the mobility we gain through all the mobile devices. And by, I think 2015, some two-thirds of the population were living in urban areas.

Jan Boelen
Bringing nature back into …

Maria Jeglinska
Into our daily lives. The idea is to present planters, as well a side table/stool, and they're quite flexible in how they can be used. I was quite inspired by a company created in the 1950s in California called 'Architecture Pottery'. A couple that started promoting outdoor life indoors, like in offices and the home by creating this beautiful set of planters made by very famous ceramicists. There're a lot of parallels today to how the Californian lifestyle has spread across the world, especially in Europe, through Google or Instagram, who are also based there …

Jan Boelen
OK. Commonplace Studio, Jon Stam. You're also connecting the ideas of the digital world with the real world. We can see your ottomans here in the front.

Jon Stam
Yes, we called them Commonplace Ottomans, so just ordinary, normal ottomans. And we were typecast actually before starting this project. We were asked to do something for the *Communals*, and we decided to create the furniture as the 'community'. We tried to see how we can give them a little bit of life, a little bit of a mind of their own, so sometimes they congregate, sometimes they wander off. They are humans …

Jan Boelen
They also fight?

Jon Stam
Yes, they could potentially bump.

Jan Boelen
Can we hack them?

Jon Stam
(laughs) Possibly, yes.

Jan Boelen
OK, great. And Jay, what do we see here from you?

Jay Osgerby
We have two things in the exhibition—a fantastic exhibition, I might add. One is this piece in white, which is part of the *Communals* section and we also have the Tip Ton chair in the *Restless* section. The white object is a kind of preview of something that we have been working on for a couple of years. It is a project which has grown out of the changes we have seen in society, which have changed the way that we work together communally, and how the office is really vanishing from our lives.

Jan Boelen
As for me, when I heard about the *Typecasting* project for the first time, I was, and I am intrigued by the work of Robert Stadler, who is always bringing a kind of idea, philosophy or attitude relating to the digital world to bear in order to question everyday life, everyday life objects. And I would like to start with the images. Here we have 'You Name It'. A shelf? This is really an object as an actor. It's really representing another world. What do we see?

Robert Stadler
We indeed see a shelf with a strange object sitting on it. You name it is an expression meaning 'whatever you want' implying 'whatever you want it to be'. There is one part of the shelf, the actual shelf, which is a sleek, geometrically controlled object. It is real, we could even say very real, because we sanded the wood so that its natural grain is enhanced. It stands for the comprehensible world of physical objects. And then there is this other part, a kind of splash that looks like a random shape, as if something has gone wrong in this perfect world. And this part–despite its looks–is actually not made of wood. It's a fake, an illusion made with a quite interesting technique named hydrographic printing. This process allows you to apply

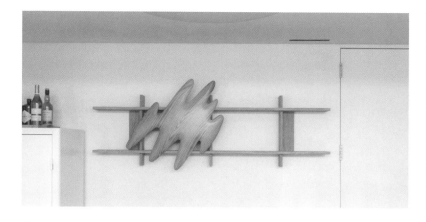

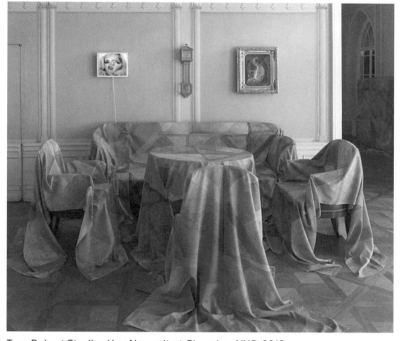

Top: Robert Stadler, You Name It at Chamber NYC, 2016;
Bottom: Robert Stadler, Back in 5 min, MAK Design Salon #3 exhibition, 2014

Top: Barber & Osgerby, Olympic torch, London 2012;
Bottom: Edward Barber & Jay Osgerby, Pacific Chair, Vitra 2016

patterns–in this case a wood texture–onto 3D objects of whatever material.

Jan Boelen
OK, here is another actor, and effective décor, I would call it. An image or an installation that functions as décor.

Robert Stadler
This is part of my 'Back In Five Minutes' solo show which took place at the Geymüllerschlössel, a branch of the MAK, the Museum of Applied Art and Contemporary Art in Vienna. The old Biedermeier mansion in Vienna's cottage district was previously owned by a watch collector. The place has an awkward feeling because there are 150 watches displayed, all standing still. Also there are these ghost-like dust covers that people once placed over the furniture before they travelled. We reproduced the patterns of the various floors in the villa and printed them on new textiles incorporating some disturbances. These blurry zones are a reproduction of the previsualisation of what happens on Google Earth during the moment when the image is loading. And it's actually a moment in two ways: the moment of the calculation of the rendering and the

moment in history which soon will not exist anymore, as computers will be fast enough so the image will just pop up instantly.

Jan Boelen
No more glitches soon, great. Thank you, Robert.
The next image is the Torch. It's the ultimate object that functions or is in fact a prop for an actor itself …

Jay Osgerby
It could be a prop. It's an object which was not chosen by the people it represents, namely the athletes or the nation but by the IOC. It was a quite stressful project, because it had to stay alight for 70 days with 4.2 billion people watching it on TV. I'm not quite sure what that makes it, but it's certainly a unique project.

Jan Boelen
The most broadcast object you ever created.

Jay Osgerby
That's probably true. It's kind of half trophy, half piece of sporting equipment. So, I love it. And it conveyed a lot of narrative, it carried a lot of meaning within the design.

Barber & Osgerby, Ballot Chair for Isokon Plus, 2017

Jan Boelen
Next image. What do we see here? Here is something that is maybe not real.

Jay Osgerby
This is an abstract illustration that we did as an invitation when we were launching the Pacific Chair for Vitra. Quite a lot of the work that we do is based on drawing, sketching, examining shapes and developing them through model-making. That's why we felt it was appropriate, in this case, to use abstract forms to try and give an indication of what was coming.

Jan Boelen
You have a strategy to do that regularly?

Jay Osgerby
No, it isn't conscious actually. This time it was a conscious decision, partly because the project wasn't complete and partly because it was about promoting a sense of the intriguing. But the images that we've looked at so far are ones for which we've used Instagram and they come after the event. We haven't used Instagram to promote something. So it's retrospective. We are actually using it as a kind of archiving, or recording method.

Jan Boelen
So, it's research space, too? You are looking back at yourself then?

Jay Osgerby
It's more like a website but I consider it a parallel world. I don't see it as something that's a real part of reality.

Jan Boelen
And you are involved in doing it yourself?

Jay Osgerby
No. Actually, Ed does most of it. Maybe that's why. Maybe I'm too sceptical. (laughs)

Jan Boelen
OK, good. Next image. What do we see here? It's a glitch.

Jay Osgerby
That is the back of the Ballot Chair. So that is mid-process, again, which is something that is important to us.

Jan Boelen
And, why do you share something like that?

Jay Osgerby
Because we regularly talk about the process being important to our studio. In a way, this demystifies the fact that objects just come out of nowhere. Especially the younger generation thinks increasingly that you can go online, press a button, and the object simply arrives. People don't necessarily have an appreciation of the effort that goes into creating something. Not only do we show this type of thing on our Instagram account, but we have also done an exhibition called 'In the Making' where we stopped the process of production along the way for that very reason. To try and make ... When we were kids, we felt that making was a magical process, and our feeling is that people have become disassociated or disengaged from it. So, it's important to try and restate the importance and also the enjoyment of this aspect.

Jan Boelen
OK, next image, Front.

Sofia Lagerkvist
This project started as a research project. We interviewed more than 100 people in their homes about their belongings, what kind of objects they loved, and what kind of objects they hated. We got all kinds of stories why they kept certain objects that no longer worked. That was quite a while ago, and there were not that many figurative objects then, I would say. Vitra has a real history of figurative objects. What we realised when we visited people's homes was that they were often very attached to figurative things. Or saw something figurative in objects like, 'Oh, that coffee machine looks like a person.' Or they had names for certain objects, and so on.

Front Design, The Animal Thing for Mooi, 2006

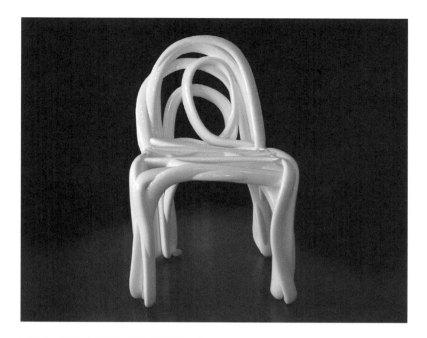

Jan Boelen
This project, is still ongoing, right? It essentially makes or promotes itself, doesn't it?

Anna Lindgren
Yes, this was 2003, so before Instagram. It started with people sending us photos of themselves. Riding a horse, or wedding photos for the whole world to see. People really hated or loved this object. Later on we posted it on Instagram and it turned out to be a selfie type of object even if that was never the purpose. So we have had Usain Bolt posting himself with the horse, Madonna, and it was in Robin William's wedding photo. It's interesting when something sort of takes on a little life of its own.

Jan Boelen
Would you consider to start designing something solely with a view to the selfie? In 2003, the selfie was not there, this is happening now. Would you now start designing for the sake of the selfie itself?

Anna Lindgren
I don't know. It wouldn't be the main purpose, but a lot of designers now are aware that things do end up on Instagram. And today in Milan, there are a lot of exhibitions that have laid things out such as to be easy to post online. And lots of objects exist as pictures, more than as real objects. Many things in this exhibition most people have only seen as pictures and today we can see them all interacting together, and that's amazing.

Jan Boelen
Almost as real pictures. 3D pictures. OK, next picture. What do we see?

Sofia Lagerkvist
This is a project called Sketch Furniture, which is a miniature now in the Vitra Design Museum. It has just been released, during this Salon, something we are very excited about.

Top: Front Design, Sketch Furniture Performance Design, 2007;
Bottom: Design, Sketch Furniture Performance Design, Pre-performance and 3D explosion, 2007

Jan Boelen
Is this the real one, or is it the miniature? We can't actually tell.

Sofia Lagerkvist
As you can't see the scale, no. It was created as a digital image to start with, because we used a digital technique. We were drawing the object in the air, and we were working with motion capture to seize the gesture. Then we created a digital file that we could print in 3D. And this was in 2003. I think until then the idea of combining these two techniques had never been done before, and we wanted to create a tool where it was possible to sketch directly in the air, and also as designers to visualise something. And we wanted to capture that direct and intuitive process.

Jan Boelen
So here you are also staging yourself. You become part of the design here. Next image.

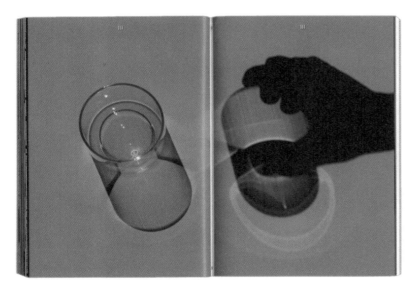

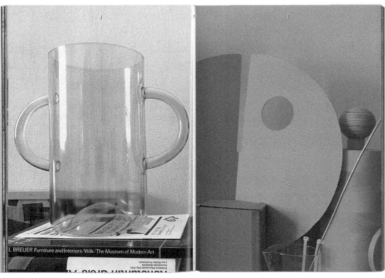

Maria Jeglinska, Space Time publication, Published by Villa Noailles, Hyères 2018. Photography by Katrin Greiling

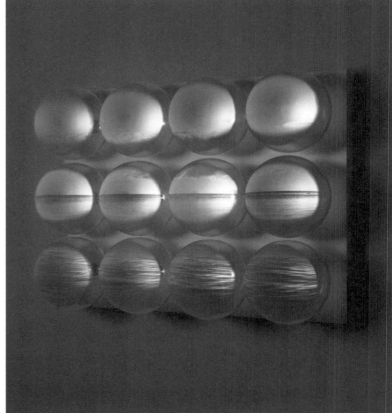

Top: Maria Jeglinska, Circles tables, 2016;
Bottom: Commonplace Studio, Lumière – wall, 2015

Sofia Lagerkvist
Here, we were invited by Moooi Carpets to design a rug to be made using a very high-end printing technique. We thought that we'd draw a sketch of a rug that would then be printed. So it was all about reintroducing the craft of making a rug into this digital technique.

Jan Boelen
Real, unreal, fictional—our own fictions, are continuously part of your work, you could say. They are almost the driving forces. Now let's go back to Maria Jeglinska.

Maria Jeglinska
This is the book publication about my work, which is called 'Space Time', and it was released in conjunction with a small, monographic exhibition I had at the Villa Noailles. I thought it would be interesting, rather than showing a fixed exhibition to instead show a work in progress. The exhibition was created through three frontal representations, which were construed almost like film stills. The film started within the four walls of the office and then moved onto other projects. There's a silent voice, in the form of subtitles that guides you

throughout the book and tells you the story of the office, its space, the projects, and the themes that drive the work behind. The film ends with a series of images on the idea of viewing objects as prosthesis, as extensions of our own bodies, rather than seeing them as separate entities.

Jan Boelen
OK. Next image.

Maria Jeglinska
These are tables, a side table and a small coffee table called Circles. It was actually my diploma project from 2007 which was about–and this is something that perhaps represents the essence of one of the themes

Commonplace Studio, Paper Mirror at Dutch Invertuals, DDW 2017

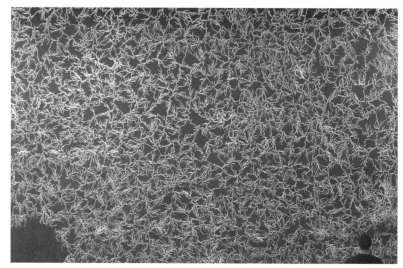

Ronan & Erwan Bouroullec, Algue for Vitra, 2004. Photography by Paul Tahon

in my practice–reducing the elements constituting the object. The idea was to reduce the object to its bare minimum through the verbs that constitute the object. Like supporting, placing and holding.

Jan Boelen
Next image. Jon Stam, Commonplace Studio.

Jon Stam
In our practice, we're trying to take what is actually beautiful about Instagram, and how that becomes a material object again. So we are often trying to frame digital things, and make them more a physical experience. This is a series called 'Lumiere': luminaires where we built in tiny projectors instead of a normal lamp fixture. You get these sublime images that could totally be someone's 10-second clip on Instagram. We went to a lake in the Netherlands, or rather what once was the sea in the Netherlands, where the light quality is super nice. We shot at different points of the day, so basically, in the morning, you see the sunrise, and at night you see the sunset. The purpose is to be not narrative at all so people would ask, 'Where is this?' and that's the point: You try to think of where this could be or where you remember this almost clichéd experience, but it's still quite stunning.

Jan Boelen
OK. Next image.

Jon Stam
This a black piece of paper (laughs) in a glass box, with a little reflective coating on it. We often work with complex technologies, but we basically see technology as a tool, and also really just a material. And for us, a piece of black paper can be just as wonderful as working on a robot inside of an ottoman.

Jan Boelen
Next image.

Erwan Bouroullec
That's not me, that's my brother's Instagram.

Jan Boelen
Nevertheless, I think this gesture, this drawing of a certain movement is really a part of the fascination.

Erwan Bouroullec
I think one of the very strong keys in design is to eliminate things, all the time. What is strange is that when you start to develop something, you know that the best thing you can do is to remove things from inside. So that things really end up like having no idea. Don't put anything more inside, or it will be corrupted. I think in our case it seems simple, but if you look for example at Jonathan Ive and Apple… I believe that Apple made very similar designs for maybe 15 years and when you repeat the same thing, you do it better, and better. This is the real performance that sometimes a product has to achieve. Somehow you need to enter into a certain say meditation ... Anyhow in my case when I'm drawing or making mock-ups, just repeating very similar things, that is one way of removing things.

Jan Boelen
That's the complete opposite of the very accelerated digital world. The next image is a nice one I think …

Erwan Bouroullec
I think design is very problematic, because on the one hand, we need new solutions and–even if it sounds ridiculous– a performance. Design is part of production, it's industry, it's numbers, it's consuming, it needs rationality. And at the same time, we also need to find

new patterns. Design is not exactly the motor of change, but sometimes, it's a sign of change and sometimes it's real change. When sneakers were invented, for example, it was crucially important for healthy exercise. But when Verner Panton made his chair for example, he didn't invent anything, but it still helped a lot of people say, 'This thing exists, I am thinking differently, and things are gonna change.' What I want to say is a part of design is only the expression of something. Then you have to do the good work and make sure it's well-produced. But at the end it's about expressing. Expressing change sometimes can look ridiculous. You might say: 'So why would I spend time doing these Algues, they're totally useless. But maybe, their function is to say, 'Let's change the rules', or, at least, 'What are the rules?'

Jan Boelen
Next image, no rules, it's almost like unreal, but it's real. It is playing with scale, too. It's how that one thing can be used…

Erwan Bouroullec
One way to change the rules is to make the rules disappear like this cloud we've been doing. It is a shape with no roots. You don't know where it comes from; you can't really connect to it. It doesn't remind you of a piece of wood or a piece of bread or something you've seen. So, since you don't remember, you can't connect it to a tradition. In the pieces by Front for example, the way they bring animals, is a very strong way to connect to some kind of roots. Because then the brain is totally at ease, because it's making an opposition between the live animals and the function, and the objects become very powerful. And then there is the other way, which is for example Dan Flavin where you can't connect to scale, you can't connect to the practice, and it makes you operate in a different way. And, so, this exhibition has a lot of this. It's about shapes that try to erase the rules.

Jan Boelen
Thank you. Thank you everybody, thank you Robert, thank all of you here and … We are all characters!

Q&A
Robert Stadler with

Jan Boelen
Simon Denny
Eva Franch i Gilabert
Front/Sofia Lagerkvist
and Anna Lindgren
Konstantin Grcic
Lena Henke
Hella Jongerius
Mark Lee
Jasper Morrison
Jonathan Muecke
Jonathan Olivares
Alice Rawsthorn

An object's display is more important than ever and we have become insatiable image consumers. How do you think this affects the status of the actual object? Will we always long for it? Could the permanent flow of images satisfy our need for consumption and the new?

Jan Boelen
Our society is definitely heading towards an increase in the consumption of information over objects. Therefore we shouldn't hold on to a design entangled in a modern, material culture. The consumption of images, the greed for the new is a facet of our society that design has to take into account. Nowadays it is time to imagine design as a practice that maps, intervenes and challenges existing processes and repurposes them towards other (more exciting) ends. The object and its image, its semiotics, shouldn't be considered separately. They are one aggregate of data that can be used, consumed, and recycled in many different ways.

Simon Denny
Images are objects, and display and physicality will be more granular and contextual with new devices and interfaces in emergent tech. Also, I'm not sure I agree with the implied idea that people need to consume new things. It doesn't have to be that way.

Eva Franch i Gilabert
I do not conflate images and objects. The image for me has its own objecthood beyond the object that it represents.

Front
The world will never tire of images, and modern history tells us that novelty never goes out of fashion. In our work we have always been interested in the interplay of an object and its image. In 2005 we made a video game as a medium through which to experience objects in new ways. It was a physics sandbox that allowed you to manipulate objects in a digital world. Today we see the logical conclusion of this speculation: Through new digital media, the boundary between the object and its image will blur and disappear.

Lena Henke
The proliferation of desires will surely increase, and we will be more educated viewers in the future. We will always need, and in needing and responding to our new stimuli overload will become more informed, sensitive, and responsive. We need to end nihilism and fight fatigue and apathy, and ask more of the viewer; therefore I want to believe that we will be always be open to something new.

Mark Lee
Designers today often overindulge in visual display, screaming at their audience to submit to their own experience. At a time when there is much more information available than attention, the role of display should be to edit out visual cacophony–like a good mystery, slowly revealing the plot to those who give the object the time and attention that it demands.

Jasper Morrison
I think many designers and manufacturers have realised the importance of good photography and presentation of their work and how important it is to promote their designs in a highly competitive market. A really good image of a product can have a lasting effect on a product. (Christine Keeler sitting backwards in Arne Jacobsen's chair plywood shell chair!)

Jonathan Muecke
An actual object offers a position–in relativity–in space. We may recognise that object in an image but we do not know that object as an image.

Jonathan Olivares
Photography of an object or space is a work in itself, independent of the object or space. The photograph is not the object. Joseph Kosuth's 1965 One and Three Chairs makes this abundantly clear. I reject the flow of images. No Instagram. No online magazines. I only read printed magazines in bulk, for example going through 50 years of Interior Design or 30 years of Thrasher. I made a commitment years ago to buy books and spend time in libraries, and be very conscious of the kind of images I spend time with. Producing and seeing new work is important and enjoyable, but equally important is the historical material. I reject the consumption of images–propagated by the Silicon Valley culture that aims to accelerate, profit, and commoditise our imagery–and would advise anyone who wants to maintain a meaningful relationship with visual material to do the same.

Alice Rawsthorn
Living in a relentless blizzard of visual imagery has, inevitably, affected our relationship to objects. Whether or not it does so adversely is determined entirely by the quality of an object's design. If a thing is poorly designed, for whatever reason, we will be more likely to forget it, and to do so faster, than we would have done pre-social media. The more thoughtfully, imaginatively and responsibly designed an object is, the greater the chances of it playing a meaningful and lasting role in our lives.

The influence of likes and comments on social media promotes certain designs against others that are less popular. Digital technology increasingly provides insights into consumer behaviour and in fields such as fashion, the production of goods is adapted almost in real time. Which effect could such instant feedback and anticipation have on design?

Jan Boelen

Design has the powerful faculty to create new meaning. Simulation, resistance, reappropriation and negotiation are only a few of the strategies designers with a critical attitude can apply to produce other narratives, what one might call a form of critical imagineering. Not only is it necessary to undo what exists, but also to design and reconfigure the normative relationships between things such as contracts, protocols, mediation, communication flows, and social or digital encounters.

Simon Denny

Automated systems which collate and classify data from these feedback systems may increasingly define what is produced/justified. If companies believe that amassed data accurately describes what people want, then it's likely they will produce along these lines. Classification systems are always biased and automated systems reproduce bias faster and in greater volumes than those where more steps involve human decision-making, so it's likely that the principles that exist in design today will be further entrenched in the future. Regardless of whether a system emerges of custom-produced micro-designs or not, with differing materials and processes, centralised systems of data analysis will likely skew decision-making powers and influence towards those who define what counts as relevant feedback wherever those people are involved in the process.

Eva Franch i Gilabert

It seems as if you are talking of a creative rationale existing without a creative impulse. There is always something irrational–creative–in the processing of information, of 'likes', of trends, of cities, of lives, of stories.

Front

The instant feedback culture that so profoundly influences production in fashion does not yet work in the same way in the design world. There are, of course, many companies that use Amazon data and analyses of social media to identify commercial opportunities for new products. But to develop a design project like the ones we do with a serious company takes a long time, the process is often secret, and it involves a long and gradual exchange of ideas between a designer and a producer. It is not so easy to see how social media 'likes' can or should influence that cultural exchange.

Konstantin Grcic

Design, which follows consumer behaviour produces obvious solutions to obvious problems. If design was seriously driven by majority vote, it would soon start to bore consumers with products they already know and make them look for something else. The magic of design is that it can be radical and unpredictable and daring to look beyond what is commonly desired.

Lena Henke

I want to resist this bottom-up searching for an instantly available, always online, never-out-of-reach one-liner, in favour of full context and depth.

Mark Lee

While instant feedback expedites the design process, there is an intrinsic value to being slow, embracing delay, and being off pace. A case in point: Scandinavia's commitment to classical architecture in the earlier part of the 20th century resulted in the delayed arrival of Modernism. When the movement did arrive, it was already a more refined and mature Modernism than what had transpired in western Europe.

Jasper Morrison

It may be something like an expanded and perpetual Milan Fiera!

Jonathan Muecke

It could narrow our expectation of objects to only address what we directly ask of them.

Jonathan Olivares

In my design process, none.

All the above-mentioned phenomena are mainly made possible through algorithms. Do you think an algorithm could be a designer's or artist's competitor? If not, what would be his/her 'added value'?

Jan Boelen
The future is where a product becomes a process, a narrative a performance; creating an unpredictable reality of a cloud, a ghost like an algorithm that knows what you might like. Rather than being governed by these ghosts, like puppets in a spectacle, we need to become the active actors on the stage.

Simon Denny
As an algorithm is simply an automated process, many parts of industry today rely on protocols that behave algorithmically–be they social conventions or material processes or otherwise. I think these are not able to compete with designers, because they do not do what designers do, they are in fact themselves designed. So it could be that the role of the designer/artist shifts to being the ones responsible for feeding and producing algorithms, but that is not the same thing as being in competition with designers/artists.

Eva Franch i Gilabert
What is becoming apparent is that that the *author* has never been the author. Call it an algorithm or zeitgeist, art exists in the eye of the beholder, in the cultural context that constructs it.

Front
There is no designer who has not googled a reference, so in that way algorithms are already our assistants. Every cultural product today exists within the hierarchies and hyperlinks that are created by automatic digital processes. However, Google still needs Bjarke Ingels to design their campus and Apple still needs Jonny Ive. We are not worried yet.

Konstantin Grcic
Algorithms can play a role in a creative process ... not as a competitor, but as a tool helping the designer. In such a scenario, the designer is still the mastermind of the operation. His/her authorship adds an irreplaceable value to any project, making it be more than just the sum of its parts.

Lena Henke
No, I prefer the handmade over the A.I. and I'll take it's human flaws anytime.

Mark Lee
Algorithms are important and necessary tools for design, but insofar as they remain tools. As C.S. Lewis once said, 'The thing that tells you which note on the piano needs to be played louder cannot itself be that note.'

Jonathan Muecke
Since we cannot read each other's minds we will always value the output of that mind….

Jonathan Olivares
Algorithms can be extremely useful within the design process. For the designer and the user design is about human enjoyment–it exists at the top of Maslow's hierarchy of need. I doubt that algorithms enjoy themselves. Efficiency and so-called 'added value' commoditise human activity, which I am firmly against. Should computation ever gain consciousness I would love to collaborate with it.

Alice Rawsthorn
Algorithms already exert great influence over various areas of daily life, including design, whether we are aware of it or not. Their influence is sure to intensify in future, creating a doughty challenge–and intriguing opportunity–for design to help to ensure that they affect us positively, rather than negatively. Thus far, many of the problems posed by algorithms stem from their retrospective nature, because their analyses are based on historical data. This has been identified as a principal cause of recent algorithmic debacles, such as the racist bias of PredPol, the crime predictive software used by US police departments, and the anti-Semitic abuse relayed by Microsoft's chatbot, Tay. Adopting a more intelligent and sensitive approach to the design of algorithms, and to anticipating their impact, should help us to make the most of their power in anticipating our needs and wishes more subtly and precisely, while avoiding their dangers. Algorithms are tools, and their success or failure will be determined by how smartly they are used.

YPECASTING

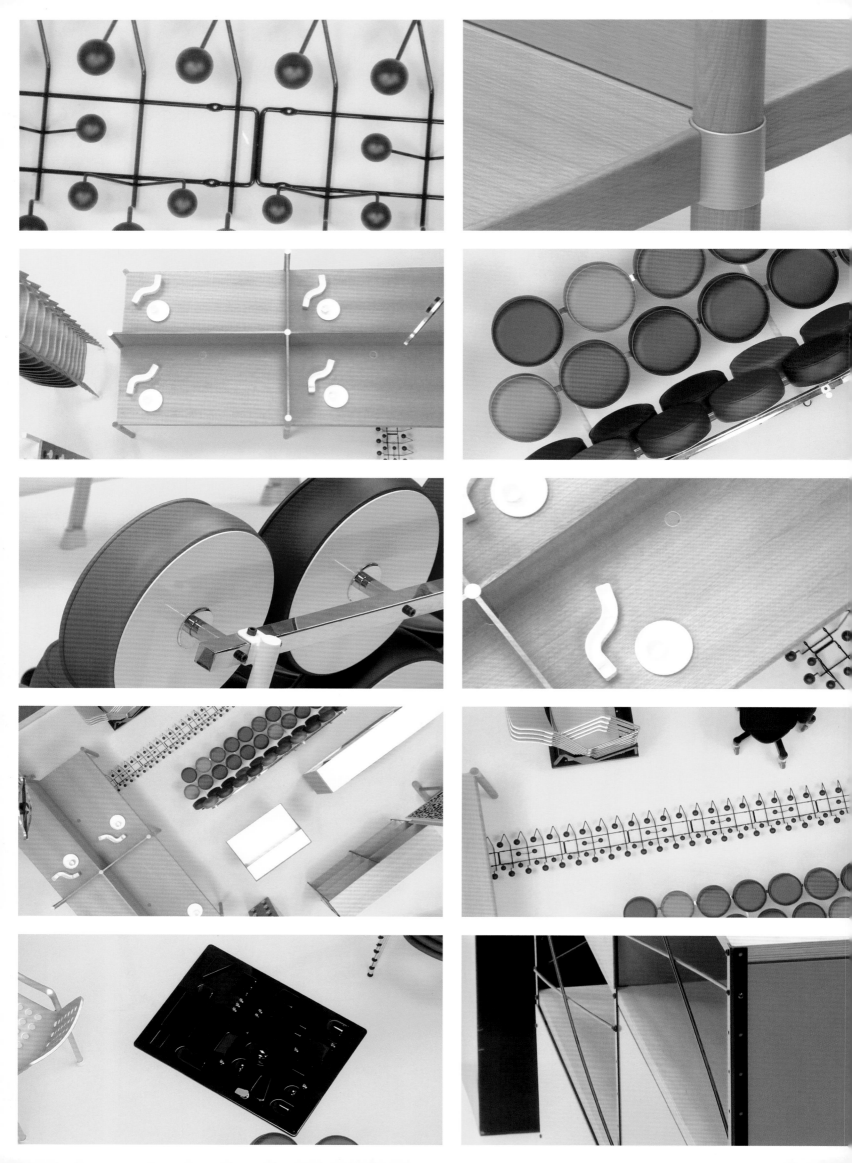

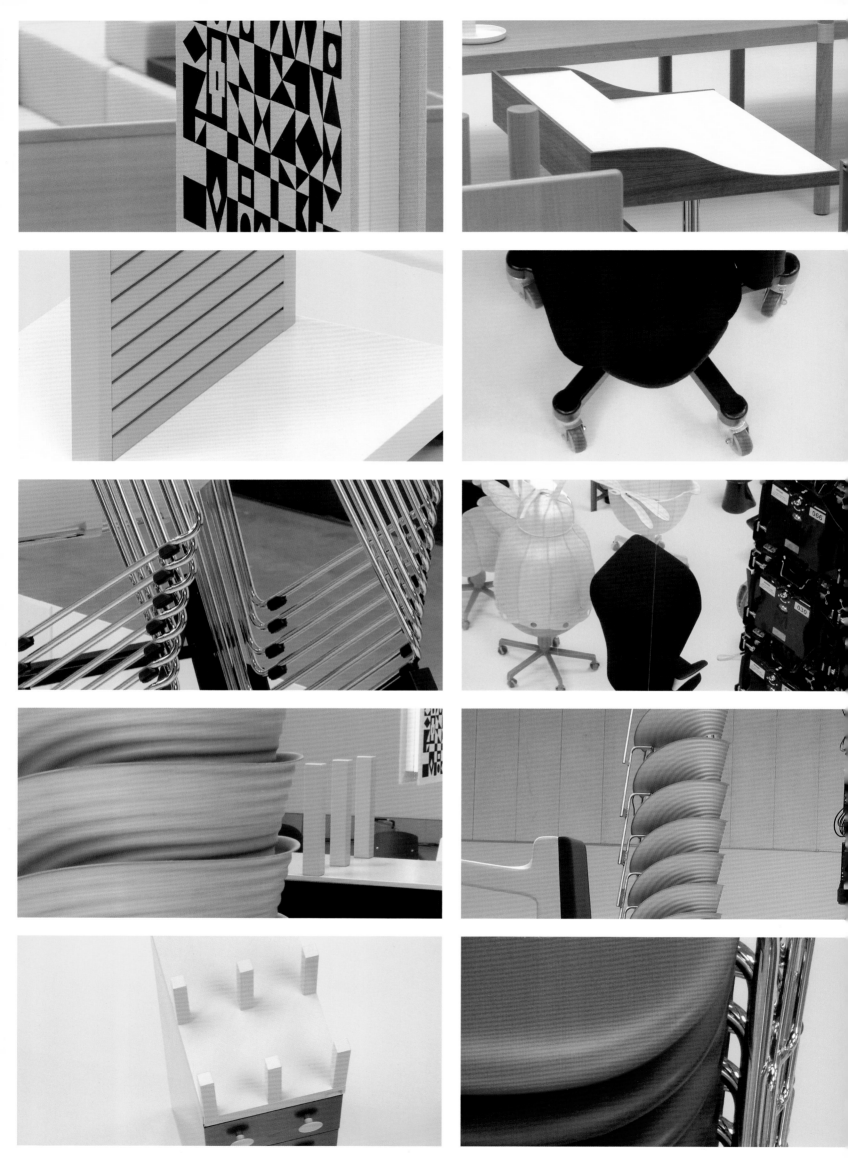

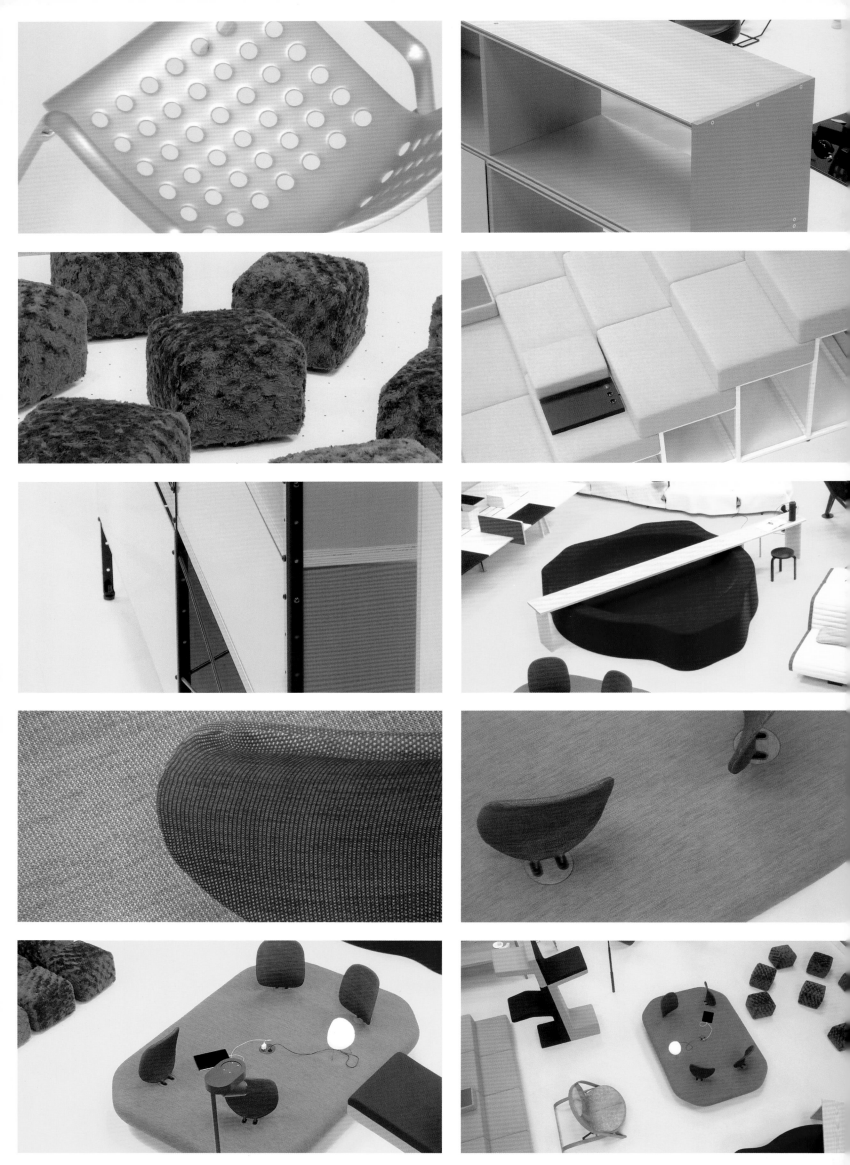

TYPECASTING

Biographies

Edward Barber & Jay Osgerby Edward Barber, born in Shrewsbury in 1969, and Jay Osgerby, born in Oxford in 1969, studied architecture and interior design as fellow students at the Royal College of Art in London. In 1996, they founded their own studio for design and architecture under the name Barber & Osgerby. Since that time, their collaborative work has probed the interface between industrial design, furniture design and architecture.

Jan Boelen is artistic director of Z33 House for Contemporary Art in Hasselt, Belgium, artistic director of Atelier Luma, Luma's's experimental laboratory for design in Arles, France, and curator of the 4th Istanbul Design Biennial (22 Sep–4 Nov 2018) in Istanbul, Turkey. He also holds the position of the head of the Master department Social Design at Design Academy Eindhoven in the Netherlands.

Studio Bouroullec Ronan (born 1971) and Erwan Bouroullec (born 1976) are brothers and designers based in Paris. They have been working together for about fifteen years bonded by diligence and challenged by their distinct personalities. Their studio is based in Paris and their team numbers around six people. Their work has covered many field ranging from the design of small objects as jewellery to spatial arrangements and architecture, from craftsmanship to industrial scale, from drawings to videos and photography. The designers also maintain an experimental activity with Gallery kreo, which is also essential to the development of their work.

Commonplace Studio is the Dutch design practice of designer **Jon Stam**, born in 1984 in Canada, and the hardware and software engineer **Simon de Bakker**, born in 1979 in the Netherlands. In their work they focus on accessible new technologies for the social and aesthetic demands of the domestic sphere and implement their projects with context-driven objects, quality craftsmanship and quiet interactions.

Simon Denny is an artist working with installation, sculpture and video. He studied at the University of Auckland, and at the Städelschule, Frankfurt am Main and since 2018 is a professor of time-based media at the HFBK Hamburg. Selected solo exhibitions include: MOCA, Cleveland (2018); OCAT, Shenzhen (2017); Hammer Museum, Los Angeles (2017); WIELS Contemporary Art Centre, Brussels (2016); Serpentine Galleries, London (2015); MoMA PS1, New York (2015) and Portikus, Frankfurt (2014). Selected group shows include: Hello World – For the Post-Human Age, Art Tower Mito (2018); Unfinished Conversations, The Museum of Modern Art, New York (2017); The 9th Berlin Biennale (2016); Hack Space, K11 Art Foundation, Hong Kong (2016). Denny represented New Zealand at the 56th Venice Biennale (2015).

Rolf Fehlbaum is Chairman Emeritus of Vitra.

In 2018 **Eva Franch i Gilabert** decided to stop writing her bio. She is the Director of the Architecture Association School of Architecture in London.

Sofia Lagerkvist and **Anna Lindgren**–both from Sweden–founded the Stockholm-based design–studio **Front** in 2004. Their work constantly questions the design process, whether through their 'collaborations' with animals, magicians, artisans or through their experiments with advanced technology. They have designed objects for major design brands across the world and are represented by Galerie Kreo in Paris and Friedman Benda in New York. Their work is in the collection of Vitra Design Museum, MoMA, Centre Pompidou and the Victoria & Albert Museum.

Konstantin Grcic trained as a cabinetmaker at the John Makepeace School in Dorset, England, before studying industrial design at the Royal College of Art in London. Since founding his Munich-based practice Konstantin Grcic Industrial Design (KGID) in 1991, he has developed products, furniture and lighting for leading design companies. Many of Grcic's products have received international design awards and his work can also be found in the permanent collections of important design museums (such as MoMA, New York, and Centre Georges Pompidou, Paris). He has curated a number of design exhibitions, including DESIGN REAL for the Serpentine Gallery, London (2009), COMFORT for the Saint-Etienne Design Biennale (2010) and black2 for the Istituto Svizzero in Rome (2010). In 2012 he was responsible for the exhibition design of the German Pavilion at the 13th Architecture Biennale in Venice. In 2018 the design of the exhibition Night Fever. Designing Club Culture 1960–Today at the Vitra Design Museum.

Lena Henke (born 1982 in Warburg (GER)) lives and works in New York City. Henke has studied at the Städelschule under Professor Michael Krebber. Henke has developed a diverse body of sculptural works, often arranged in comprehensive spatial installations. Henke's work references urban planning, Land Art, human relationships, sexuality and fetishism, consistently infiltrating the patriarchal structure of art history with a very smart and humorous tone. Her formal language and use of materials often alludes to Minimal Art combined vividly with Surrealist imagery to examine the structures of street life and the ideas of city planners and urban theorists such as Jane Jacobs, Roberto Burle Marx, and Robert Moses. Recent solo exhibitions have been presented internationally at venues including Kunsthalle Zurich, (2018); Schirn Kunsthalle Frankfurt, Sprengelmuseum Hannover, Germany (both 2017). Henke's work has been included in group exhibitions at institutions including the Whitney Museum of Art, (2018); Bard Hessel Museum, New York; (2018). Her work has been featured in major international exhibitions including the Timisoara Contemporary Art Biennale, Romania, (2017); Manifesta 11, Zurich, Switzerland (2016); The 9th; Berlin Biennale, Germany (2016); Le Biennale de MONTREAL, Montreal, Canada, (2016); and The New Museums Triennial, New Museum, New York (2015). Henkes work is included in the permanent collection of the Whitney Museum of Modern Art in New York, the Sammlungsverbund Wien in Austria, and at the Skulpturen Museum Glaskaten Marl in Germany.

Maria Jeglinska, born in 1983 in Fontainebleau, France, graduated from ECAL's industrial design course in 2007 and was awarded a scholarship from the IKEA foundation that led to her work for the Kreo Gallery in Paris, Konstantin Grcic in Munich and Alexander Taylor in London. In 2010 Maria Jeglinska founded a studio for design and research in London. Her projects are guided by the conviction that research and design can generate new types of answers and possibilities in today's world.

Hella Jongerius The Dutch designer Hella Jongerius lives and works in Berlin. She founded the Jongeriuslab studio in 1993 and began collaborating with Vitra in 2004. Since then, she has not only contributed a substantial number of designs to the continually expanding Vitra Home Collection, but has also applied her expertise in the realm of colours and materials to the Vitra Colour & Material Library.

Mark Lee is the Chair of the Department of Architecture at the Harvard Graduate School of Design and a founding partner of the architecture firm Johnston Marklee and Associates. Projects undertaken by Johnston Marklee include the Menil Drawing Institute and the UCLA Graduate Art Studios. Together with Sharon Johnston, Lee was the Artistic Director for the 2017 Chicago Architecture Biennial.

Jasper Morrison Born in London, 1959, studied Design at Kingston Polytechnic, The Royal College of Art and the Hochschule der Kunst in Berlin. Opened an Office for Design in London, 1986. Designs different things in London, Paris and Tokyo, works for Vitra, Flos, Muji, Emeco, Cappellini Magis and others. Published several books with Lars Müller Publishers. Worked on a variety of exhibitions at his shop in London and in museums and galleries around the world.

Jonathan Muecke resists standard divisions between design, art and architecture, instead focusing on refined forms that investigate notions of positive and negative space, positional relationships to structures and the innate desire to read notions of functionality into objects that relate to human scale. His works are in the collections of several museums including The Museum of Art and Design in New York City, San Francisco Museum of Modern Art, Center National des Arts Plastiques in Paris, the Musée des Arts Décoratifs in Montreal, and The Art Institute of Chicago.

Jonathan Olivares was born in Boston in 1981 and graduated from Pratt Institute. In 2006 he established his practice, which is based in Los Angeles and works in the fields of industrial, spatial and communication design. His designs engage a legacy of form and technology, and ask to be used rather than observed. Recent projects include the installation Room for a Daybed (2016); the Aluminum Bench, for Zahner (2015); the Vitra Workspace, an office furniture showroom and learning environment for Vitra (2015); the exhibition Source Material, curated with Jasper Morrison and Marco Velardi (2014); and the Olivares Aluminum Chair, for Knoll (2012). Olivares' work has been published internationally, granted several design awards—including Italy's Compasso d'Oro—and is included in the permanent design collections of the Art Institute of Chicago, the Los Angeles County Art Museum, The Victoria and Albert Museum, and the Vitra Design Museum.

Alice Rawsthorn is an award-winning design critic and the author of the critically acclaimed books, Design as an Attitude and Hello World: Where Design Meets Life. A founding member of the Writers for Liberty campaign to champion human rights and freedoms, she is chair of the boards of trustees at Chisenhale Gallery in London and The Hepworth Wakefield in Yorkshire.

Robert Stadler was born in 1966 in Vienna, Austria and studied design at IED/Milan and at ENSCI/Paris. In 1992 he cofounded the Radi Designers group which was active until 2008. In 2001 Robert Stadler set up his own design studio in Paris. He works for clients such as Dior, Lobmeyr, Palais de Tokyo, Ricard, Thonet and Vitra and also has created a number of limited edition pieces for Carpenters Workshop Gallery since 2008. In 2017 the Noguchi Museum in New York presented his first institutional exhibition in the US in dialogue with Isamu Noguchi's works. In the same year his first survey exhibition was shown at Kunsthalle im Lipsiusbau in Dresden, Germany. Robert Stadler has also curated several exhibitions amongst which QUIZ at Ensemble Poirel in Nancy and at MUDAM Luxemburg and Typecasting at La Pelota during Milan's Design Week 2018.

Published on the occasion of

Typecasting: An Assembly
of Iconic, Forgotten and
New Vitra Characters

at La Pelota during
Milano Design Week
April 17–22, 2018

Publication

Editor: Robert Stadler

Managing Editor: Chrissie Muhr

Graphic Design: Zak Group

Authors/Contributors:
Jay Barber and Edward
Osgerby, Jan Boelen,
Commonplace Studio/Jon
Stam and Simon de Bakker,
Simon Denny, Rolf Fehlbaum,
Eva Franch i Gilabert,
Front/Sofia Lagerkvist
and Anna Lindgren,
Konstantin Grcic, Lena Henke,
Maria Jeglinska, Hella
Jongerius, Mark Lee, Jasper
Morrison, Jonathan Muecke,
Chrissie Muhr, Jonathan
Olivares, Alice Rawsthorn,
Robert Stadler

Copyediting and Proofreading:
Barbara Hauss, Jeremy Gaines

Distribution: Dustin Cosentino

Printing: Publikum

Paper: Munken Polar 80gsm
and 130gsm, Garda Matt Art
115gsm and 300gsm

Photography:
Julien Lanoo, Mission Video

First published by
Vitra Design Museum:

Vitra Design Museum
Charles-Eames-Str. 2
79576 Weil am Rhein, Germany

Printed in Serbia

© Vitra Design Museum

ISBN 978-3-945852-29-3

Exhibition

Curator and Exhibition Design:
Robert Stadler
assisted by Théo Leclercq

Creative Direction:
Chrissie Muhr

Graphic Design: Zak Group

Exhibition Construction:
Marcin Mejsak, Mori Meana
Architects/Mateo Mori Meana
with Allestimenti Benfenati
S.p.A., Roberto Benfenati

Film/Media Technology and
Direction: Mission Video,
Ludovic Gommé, Bruno Suchy

Camera: Bruno Suchy,
Thibaut De Vreese,
Pierre-Yves Duval, Alexis Christel

Vitra would like to thank
all partners and supporters
of this exhibition:

Vitra Design Museum,
Artek, Kvadrat, Lightnet

The German National
Library has listed this
publication in the German
National Bibliography;
detailed bibliographical data
is available at http://dnb.dnb.de.